THE LORDS OF THE WILD

A Story of the Old New York Border

by

Joseph A. Altsheler

Double9
BOOKS

THE LORDS OF THE WILD
A Story of the Old New York Border
by Joseph A. Altsheler

ISBN: 978-93-57486-32-3

Published by

DOUBLE 9 BOOKS

2/13-B, Ansari Road
Daryaganj, New Delhi – 110002
info@double9books.com
www.double9books.com
Tel. 011-40042856

ABOUT THE AUTHOR

Joseph A. Altsheler was born on April 29, 1862, in Three Springs, Hart County, Kentucky, to Joseph and Louise Altsheler. He was a newspaper reporter, editor, and author of popular juvenile historical fiction. He wrote fifty novels and at least fifty-three short stories. Seven of his novels were in sequence. He worked as an editor at the Louisville Courier-Journal in 1885. In 1892, he started to work for New York World and then as the editor of the World's tri-weekly magazine. He wrote children's stories due to a lack of suitable stories. On May 30, 1880, Altsheler married Sarah Boles and had a son named Sidney. In 1914, during World War I Altsheler and his family were in Germany and they were forced to remain there. Altsheler died at the age of 57, on June 5, 1919, in New York. His wife, Sarah Boles died after 30 years. Their bodies are buried at the Cave Hill Cemetery in Louisville, Kentucky. Although each of the thirty-two novels constitutes an independent story, Altsheler suggested reading in sequence for each series (that is, he numbered the volumes). You can read the remaining eighteen novels in any order.

CONTENTS

CHAPTER I.

THE BLUE BIRD...7

CHAPTER II.

THE LIVE CANOE..20

CHAPTER III.

IN THE CLIFF...35

CHAPTER IV.

THE DARING ATTEMPT 47

CHAPTER V.

TAYOGA'S SKILL...61

CHAPTER VI.

BLACK RIFLE..75

CHAPTER VII.

THE FOREST BATTLE 87

CHAPTER VIII.

THE BOAT BUILDERS...100

CHAPTER IX.

THE MASKED ATTACK..114

CHAPTER X.

IN THE FOG...129

CHAPTER XI.

THE HAPPY ESCAPE..143

CHAPTER XII.

THE FRENCH CAMP..160

CHAPTER XIII.

EVE OF BATTLE 178

CHAPTER XIV.

TICONDEROGA 192

CHAPTER I.
THE BLUE BIRD

The tall youth, turning to the right, went down a gentle slope until he came to a little stream, where he knelt and drank. Despite his weariness, his thirst and his danger he noticed the silvery color of the water, and its soft sighing sound, as it flowed over its pebbly bed, made a pleasant murmur in his ear. Robert Lennox always had an eye for the beautiful, and the flashing brook, in its setting of deep, intense forest green, soothed his senses, speaking to him of comfort and hope.

He drank again and then sat back among the bushes, still breathing heavily, but with much more freedom. The sharp pain left his chest, new strength began to flow into his muscles, and, as the body was renewed, so the spirit soared up and became sanguine once more. He put his ear to the earth and listened long, but heard nothing, save sounds natural to the wilderness, the rustling of leaves before the light wind, the whisper of the tiny current, and the occasional sweet note of a bird in brilliant dress, pluming itself on a bough in its pride. He drew fresh courage from the peace of the woods, and resolved to remain longer there by the stream. Settling himself into the bushes and tall grass, until he was hidden from all but a trained gaze, he waited, body and soul alike growing steadily in vigor.

The forest was in its finest colors. Spring had never brought to it a more splendid robe, gorgeous and glowing, its green adorned with wild flowers, and the bloom of bush and tree like a gigantic stretch of tapestry. The great trunks of oak and elm and maple grew in endless rows and overhead the foliage gleamed, a veil of emerald lace before the sun.

Robert drank in the glory, eye and ear, but he never failed to watch the thickets, and to listen for hostile sounds. He knew full well that his life rested upon his vigilance and, often as he had been in danger in the great northern woods, he valued too much these precious days of his youth to risk their sudden end through any neglect of his own.

He looked now and then at the bird which still preened itself on a little bough. When the shadows from the waving foliage fell upon its feathers it showed a bright purple, but when the sunlight poured through, it glowed a glossy blue. He did not know its name, but it was a brave bird, a gay bird. Now and then it ceased its hopping back and forth, raised its head and sent forth a deep, sweet, thrilling note, amazing in volume to come from so small a body. Had he dared to make a sound Robert would have whistled a bar or two in reply. The bird was a friend to one alone and in need, and its dauntless melody made his own heart beat higher. If a creature so tiny was not afraid in the wilderness why should he be!

He had learned to take sharp notice of everything. On the border and in such times, man was compelled to observe with eye and ear, with all the five senses; and often too with a sixth sense, an intuition, an outgrowth of the other five, developed by long habit and training, which the best of the rangers possessed to a high degree, and in which the lad was not lacking. He knew that the minutest trifle must not escape his attention, or the forfeit might be his life.

While he relaxed his own care not at all, he felt that the bird was a wary sentinel for him. He knew that if an enemy came in haste through the undergrowth it would fly away before him. He had been warned in that manner in another crisis and he had full faith now in the caution of the valiant little singer. His trust, in truth, was so great that he rose from his covert and bent down for a third drink of the clear cool water. Then he stood up, his figure defiant, and took long, deep breaths, his heart now beating smoothly and easily, as if it had been put to no painful test. Still no sound of a foe, and he thought that perhaps the pursuit had died down, but he knew enough of the warriors of the woods to make sure, before he resumed a flight that would expose him in the open.

He crept back into the thicket, burying himself deep, and was careful not to break a twig or brush a leaf which to the unerring eyes of those who followed could mark where he was. Hidden well, but yet lying where he could see, he turned his gaze back to the bird. It was now pouring out an unbroken volume of song as it swayed on a twig, like a leaf shaken in the wind. Its voice was thrillingly sweet, and it seemed mad with joy, as its tiny throat swelled with the burden of its melody. Robert, in the thicket, smiled, because he too shared in so much gladness.

A faint sound out of the far west came to him. It was so slight that it was hard to tell it from the whisper of the wind. It barely registered on the drum of the ear, but when he listened again and with all his powers he was sure that it was a new and foreign note. Then he separated it from the breeze among the leaves, and it seemed to him to contain a quality like that of the human voice. If so, it might be hostile, because his friends, Willet, the hunter, and Tayoga, the Onondaga, were many miles away. He had left them on the shore of the lake, called by the whites, George, but more musically by the Indians, Andiatarocte, and there was nothing in their plans that would now bring them his way. However welcome they might be he could not hope for them; foes only were to be expected.

The faint cry, scarcely more than a variation of the wind, registered again though lightly on the drum of his ear, and now he knew that it came from the lungs of man, man the pursuer, man the slayer, and so, in this case, the red man, perhaps Tandakora, the fierce Ojibway chief himself. Doubtless it was a signal, one band calling to another, and he listened anxiously for the reply, but he did not hear it, the point from which it was sent being too remote, and he settled back into his bed of bushes and grass, resolved to keep quite still until he could make up his mind about the next step. On the border as well as elsewhere it was always wise, when one did not know what to do, to do nothing.

But the tall youth was keenly apprehensive. The signals indicated that the pursuing force had spread out, and it might enclose him in a fatal circle. His eager temperament, always sensitive to impressions, was kindled into fire, and his imagination painted the whole forest scene in the most vivid colors. A thought at first, it now became a conviction with him that Tandakora led the pursuit. The red leader had come upon his trail in some way, and, venomous from so many failures, would follow now for days in an effort to take him. He saw the huge Ojibway again with all the intensity of reality, his malignant face, his mighty body, naked to the waist and painted in hideous designs. He saw too the warriors who were with him, many of them, and they were fully as eager and fierce as their chief.

But his imagination which was so vital a part of him did not paint evil and danger alone; it drew the good in colors no less deep and glowing. It saw himself refreshed, stronger of body and keener of mind than ever, escaping every wile and snare laid for his ruin. It saw him making a victorious flight through the forest, his arrival at the shining lake, and his reunion with Willet and Tayoga, those faithful friends of many a peril.

He knew that if he waited long enough he would hear the Indian call once more, as the bands must talk to one another if they carried out a concerted pursuit, and he decided that when it came he would go. It would be his signal too. The only trouble lay in the fact that they might be too near when the cry was sent. Yet he must take the risk, and there was his sentinel bird still pluming itself in brilliant colors on its waving bough.

The bird sang anew, pouring forth a brilliant tune, and Robert from his covert smiled up at it again. It had a fine spirit, a gay spirit like his own and now it would surely warn him if danger crept too close. While the thought was fresh in his mind the third signal came, and now it was so clear and distinct that it indicated a rapid approach. But he was still unable to choose a way for his flight and he lingered for a sign from the bird. If the warriors were stealing through the bushes it would fly directly from them. At least he believed so, and fancy had so much power over him, especially in such a situation that belief became conviction.

The bird stopped singing suddenly, but kept his perch on the waving bough. Robert always insisted that it looked straight at him before it uttered two or three sharp notes, and then, rising in the air, hovered for a few minutes above the bough. It was obvious to him that his call had come. Steeped in Indian lore he had seen earth and air work miracles, and it was not less wonderful that a living creature should perform one now, and in his behalf.

For a breathless instant or two he forgot the warriors and watched the bird, a flash of blue flame against the green veil of the forest. It was perched there in order to be sure that he saw, and then it would show the way! With every pulse beating hard he stood up silently, his eyes still on the blue flash, confident that a new miracle was at hand.

The bird uttered three or four notes, not short or sharp now, but soft, long and beckoning, dying away in the gentlest of echoes. His imagination, as vivid as ever, translated it into a call to him to come, and he was not in the least surprised, when the blue flame like the pillow of cloud by day moved slowly to the northeast, and toward the lake. Stepping cautiously he followed his sign, thrilled at the doing of the miracle, his eyes on his flying guide, his ears attuned to warn him if any danger threatened from the forest so near.

It never occurred to Robert that he might not be led aright. His faith and confidence were supreme. He had lived too much with Tayoga not to share his belief that the hand of Manitou was stretched forth now to lead those who put their trust in him.

The blue flame that was a living bird flew slowly on, pausing an instant or two on a bough, turning for a short curve to right or left, but always coming back to the main course that pointed toward Andiatarocte.

He walked beside the little brook from which he had drunk, then across it and over a low hill, into a shallow valley, the forest everywhere, but the undergrowth not too dense for easy passage. His attentive ear brought no sound from either flank save those natural to the woods, though he was sure that a hostile call would come soon. It would be time for the bands to talk to one another. But he had no fear. The supreme intervention had been made in his favor, and he kept his eyes on his flying guide.

They crossed the valley and began the ascent of another and high hill, rough with rocky outcrops and a heavy growth of briars and vines. His pace became slower of necessity and once or twice he thought he had lost the blue flame, but it always reappeared, and, for the first time since its flight from the bough, it sang a few notes, a clear melodious treble, carrying far through the windy forest.

The lad believed that the song was meant for him. Clearly it said to him to follow, and, with equal clearness, it told him that safety lay only in the path he now traveled. He believed, with all the ardor of his soul, and there was no weariness in his body as he climbed the high hill. Near the summit, he heard on his right the long dying Indian cry so full of menace, its answer to the left, and then a third shout directly behind him. He understood. He was between the horns of a crescent, and they were not far away. He left faint traces only as he fled, but they had so much skill they could follow with speed, and he was quite sure they expected to take him. This belief did not keep his heart from beating high. They did not know how he was protected and led, and there was the blue flame before him always showing him the way. He reached the crest of the hill, and saw other hills, fold on fold, lying before him. He had hoped to catch a glimpse of the lake from the summit, but no glint of its waters came, and then he knew it must yet be miles away. His heart sank for a moment. Andiatarocte had appealed to him as a refuge. Just why he did not know, but he vaguely expected to find safety there. Perhaps he would meet Willet and Tayoga by its shore, and to him the three united always seemed invincible.

His courage was gone only an instant or two. Then it came back stronger than ever. The note of his guide, clear and uplifting, rose again, and he increased his speed, lest he be enclosed within those horns. The far slope was rocky and he leaped from one stony outcrop to another. Even if he could hide his trail only a few yards it would be so much time gained while they were compelled to seek it. He was forced to watch his steps here, but, when he was at the bottom and looked up, the blue flame was still before him. On it went over the next slope and he followed at speed, noticing with joy that the rocky nature of the ground continued, and the most skillful warrior who ever lived must spend many minutes hunting his traces. He had no doubt that he was gaining and he had proof of it in the fact that the pursuers now uttered no cry. Had they been closing in on him they would have called to one another in triumph.

Well for him that he was so strong and sound of heart and lung! Well for him too that he was borne up by a great spirit and by his belief that a supreme power was working in his behalf. He felt little weariness as he climbed a ridge. His breath was easy and regular and his steps were long and swift. His guide was before him. Whatever his pace, whether fast or slow, the distance between them never seemed to change. The bird would dart aside, perhaps to catch an insect, but it always returned promptly to its course.

His eyes caught a gleam of silver from the crest of the fourth ridge that he crossed, and he knew it was a ray of sunlight striking upon the waters of the lake. Now his coveted haven was not so far away, and the great pulses in his temples throbbed. He would reach the lake, and he would find refuge. Tandakora, in all his malice, would fail once more. The thought was so pleasant to him that he laughed aloud, and now feeling the need to use the strength he had saved with such care he began to run as fast as he could. It was his object to open up a wide gap between himself and the warriors, one so great that, if occasion came, he might double or turn without being seen.

The forest remained dense, a sea of trees with many bushes and clinging vines in which an ignorant or incautious runner would have tripped and fallen, but Robert was neither, and he did not forget, as he fled, to notice where his feet fell. His skill and presence of mind kept him from stumbling or from making any noise that would draw the attention of possible pursuers who might have crept up on his flank. While they had only his faint trail to guide them the pursuit was impeded, and, as long as they did not see him, his chance to hide was far greater.

He lost sight of his feathered guide two or three times, but the bird never failed to reappear, a brilliant blue flame against the green wall of the wilderness, his emblem of hope, leading him over the hills and valleys toward Andiatarocte. Now he saw the lake from a crest, not a mere band of silver showing through the trees, but a broad surface reflecting the sunlight in varied colors. It was a beacon to him, and, summoning the last ounce of his strength and will, he ran at amazing speed. Once more he heard the warriors behind him calling to one another, and they were much farther away. His mighty effort had not been in vain. His pulses beat hard with the throb of victory not yet won, but of which he felt sure, and he rejoiced too, because he had come again upon rocky ground, where his flight left so little trace that Tandakora himself would be baffled for a while.

He knew that the shores of the lake at the point he was nearing were comparatively low, and a vague plan to hide in the dense foliage at the water's edge came into his mind. He did not know just how he would do it, but he would be guided by events as they developed. The bird surely would not lead him on unless less to safety, and no doubt entered his mind. But it was highly important to widen yet more the distance between him and the warriors, and he still ran with all the speed at his command.

The last crest was reached and before him spread the splendid lake in its deep green setting, a glittering spectacle that he never failed to admire, and that he admired even now, when his life was in peril, and instants were precious. The bird perched suddenly on a bough, uttered a few thrilling notes, and was then gone, a last blue flash into the dense foliage. He did not see it again, and he did not expect to do so. Its work was done. Strong in the faith of the wilderness, he believed and always believed.

He crouched a few moments on a ledge and looked back. Tandakora and his men had not yet come in sight, nor could he hear them. Doubtless they had lost his trail, when he leaped from one stone to another, and were now looking for it. His time to hide, if he were to have one, was at hand, and he meant to make the most of the chance. He bent lower and remained there until his breathing became regular and easy after his mighty effort, all his five senses and the sixth that was instinct or divination, alert to every sound.

Two or three birds began to sing, but they were not his bird and he gave them no attention. A rabbit leaped from its nest under the bushes and ran. It went back on his trail and he considered it a sure sign that his pursuers were yet distant. He might steal another precious minute or two for his overworked lungs and heart. He knew the need of doing everything to gain a little more strength. It was his experience in border war and the stern training of Willet and Tayoga that made him able to do so, and he was ruler enough of himself to wait yet a little longer than he had planned. Then when he felt that Tandakora must be near, he straightened up, though not to his full height, and ran swiftly down the long slope to the lake.

He found at the bottom a narrow place between cliff and water, grown thickly with bushes, and he followed it at least half a mile, until the shores towered above him dark and steep, and the lake came up against them like a wall. He could go no farther and he waded into a dense growth of bushes and weeds, where he stood up to his waist in water and waited, hidden well.

He knew that if the warriors followed and saw him he would have little opportunity to escape, but the chances were a hundred to one against their finding him in such a covert. Rock and water had blotted out his trail and he felt safe. He secured his belt, containing his smaller weapons and ammunition, about his shoulders beyond touch of water, and put his rifle in the forks of two bushes, convenient to his hands.

It was a luxury to rest, even if one did stand half-sunken in a lake. The water was cold, but he did not yet feel the chill, and he listened for possible sounds of pursuit. He heard, after a while, the calls of warriors to one another and he laughed softly to himself. The shouts were faint and moreover they came from the crest of the cliff. They had not found his trail down the slope and they were hunting for him on the heights. He laughed again with sheer satisfaction. He had been right. Rock and water had come to his aid, and he was too well hidden even for the eager eyes of Tandakora and his warriors to follow him.

He waited a long time. He heard the cries nearer him, then farther away, and, at last, at such a great distance that they could barely be separated from the lap of the waters. He was growing cold now; the chill from the lake was rising in his body, but with infinite patience bred by long practice of the wilderness he did not stir. He knew that silence could be deceptive. Some of the warriors might come back, and might wait in a thicket, hoping that he would rise and disclose himself, thinking the danger past. More than one careless wanderer in the past had been caught in such a manner, and he was resolved to guard against the trick. Making the last call upon his patience, he stood motionless, while the chill crept steadily upward through his veins and muscles.

He could see the surface of the open lake through the veil of bushes and tall grass. The water broke in gentle waves under a light wind, and kept up a soft sighing that was musical and soothing. Had he been upon dry land he could have closed his eyes and gone to sleep, but, as it was, he did not complain, since he had found safety, if not comfort. He even found strength in himself, despite his situation, to admire the gleaming expanse of Andiatarocte with its shifting colors, and the far cliffs lofty and dim.

Much of Robert's life, much of its most eventful portion, was passing around this lake, and he had a peculiar affection for it. It always aroused in him a sense of beauty, of charm and of majesty, and he had grown too to look upon it as a friend and protector. He believed that it had brought him good luck, and he did not doubt that it would do so again.

He looked for a canoe, one perhaps that might contain Willet and Tayoga, seeking him and keeping well beyond the aim of a lurking marksman on the shore, but he saw no shadow on the water, nothing that could be persuaded into the likeness of a boat, only wild fowl circling and dipping, and, now and then, a gleam where a fish leaped up to fall swiftly back again. He was alone, and he must depend upon himself only.

He began to move a little, to lift one foot and then the other, careful to make no splash in the water, and the slight exercise checked the creeping chill. Encouraged, he increased it, stopping at intervals to listen for the approach of a foe. There was no sound and he walked back and forth a little. Presently his eyes, trained to observe all things, noticed a change in the air. A gray tint, so far a matter of quality rather than color, was coming into it, and his heart leaped with joy. Absorbed in his vital struggle he had failed to reckon the passage of time. The day was closing and blessed, covering night was at hand. Robert loved the day and the sun, but darkness was always a friend of those who fled, and now he prayed that it would come thick and dark.

The sun still hung over the eastern shores, red and blazing, but before long it went down, seeming to sink into the lake, and the night that Robert had wished, heavy and black, swept over the earth. Then he left the water, and stood upon dry land, the narrow ledge between the cliff and the waves, where he took off his lower garments, wrung them as nearly dry as he could, and, hanging them on the bushes, waited for the wind to do the rest. His sense of triumph had never been so strong. Alone and relying only upon his own courage and skill, he had escaped the fierce Tandakora and his persistent warriors. He could even boast of it to Willet and Tayoga, when he found them again.

It was wonderful to feel safe, after great peril, and his bright imagination climbed the heights. As he had escaped them then, so he would slip always from the snares of his foes. It was this quality in him, the spirit of eternal hope, that appealed so strongly to all who knew him, and that made him so attractive.

After a while, he took venison and hominy from his knapsack and ate with content. Then he resumed his clothing, now dried completely by the wind, and felt that he had never been stronger or more fitted to cope with attack.

The darkness was intense and the surface of the lake showed through it, only a fitful gray. The cliff behind him was now a black bank, and its crest could not be seen at all. He was eager to go, but he still used the patience so necessary in the wilderness, knowing that the longer he waited the less likely he was to meet the band of Tandakora.

He lay down in a thicket of tall grass and bushes, resolved not to start before midnight, and he felt so much at peace that before he knew he was going to sleep he was sleeping. When he awoke he felt a little dismay at first, but it was soon gone. After all, he had passed the time of waiting in the easiest way, and no enemy had come. The moon and stars were not to be seen, but instinct told him that it was not beyond midnight.

He arose to go, but a slight sound came from the lake, and he stayed. It was merely the cry of the night bird, calling to its mate, one would have said, but Robert's attention was attracted by an odd inflection in it, a strain that seemed familiar. He listened with the utmost attention, and when it came a second time, he was so sure that his pulses beat very fast.

Willet and Tayoga, as he had hoped in the day, were out there on the lake. It had been foolish of him to think they would come in the full sunlight, exposed to every hostile eye. It was their natural course to approach in the dark and send a signal that he would know. He imitated the call, a soft, low note, but one that traveled far, and soon the answer came. No more was needed. The circle was complete. Willet and Tayoga were on the lake and they knew that he was at the foot of the cliff, waiting.

He took a long breath of intense relief and delight. Tandakora would resume the search for him in the morning, hunting along the crest, and he might even find his way to the narrow ledge on which Robert now stood, but the lad would be gone across the waters, where he left no trail.

He saw a stout young bush growing on the edge of the lake, and, leaning far out while he held on to it with one hand, he watched. He did not repeat the call. One less cautious would have done so, but he knew that his friends had located him already and he meant to run no risk of telling the warriors also where he stood. Meanwhile, he listened attentively for the sound of the paddles, but many long minutes passed before he heard the faint dip, dip that betokened the approach of Willet and Tayoga. He never doubted for an instant that it was their canoe and again his heart felt that triumphant feeling.

Surely no man ever had more loyal or braver comrades! If he had malignant enemies he also had staunch friends who more than offset them.

He saw presently a faint shadow, a deeper dark in the darkness, and he uttered very low the soft note of the bird. In an instant came the answer, and then the shadow, turning, glided toward him. A canoe took form and shape and he saw in it two figures, which were unmistakably those of Willet and Tayoga, swinging their paddles with powerful hands. Again he felt a thrill of joy because these two trusty comrades had come. But it was absurd ever to doubt for an instant that they would come!

He leaned out from the tree to the last inch, and called in a penetrating whisper:

"Dave! Tayoga! This way!"

The canoe shifted its course a little, and entered the bushes by the side of Robert, the hunter and the Onondaga putting down their dripping paddles, and stepping out in the shallow water. In the dusk the great figure of Willet loomed up, more than ever a tower of strength, and the slender but muscular form of Tayoga, the very model of a young Indian warrior, seemed to be made of gleaming bronze. Had Robert needed any infusion of courage and will their appearance alone would have brought it with them.

"And we have found Dagaeoga again!" said the Onondaga, in a whimsical tone.

"No I have found you," said Robert. "You were lost from me, I was not lost from you."

"It is the same, and I think by your waiting here at midnight that you have been in great peril."

"So I have been, and I may be yet—and you too. I have been pursued by warriors, Tandakora at their head. I have not seen them, but I know from the venom and persistence of the pursuit that he leads them. I eluded them by coming down the cliff and hiding among the bushes here. I stood in the water all the afternoon."

"We thought you might be somewhere along the western shore. After we divided for our scout about the lake, the Great Bear and I met as we had arranged, but you did not come. We concluded that the enemy had got in the way, and so we took from its hiding place a canoe which had been left on a former journey, and began to cruise upon Andiatarocte, calling at far intervals for you."

He spoke in his usual precise school English and in a light playful tone, but Robert knew the depth of his feelings. The friendship of the white lad and the red was held by hooks of steel like that of Damon and Pythias of old.

"I think I heard your first call," said Robert. "It wasn't very loud, but never was a sound more welcome, nor can I be too grateful for that habit you have of hiding canoes here and there in the wilderness. It's saved us all more than once."

"It is merely the custom of my people, forced upon us by need, and I but follow."

"It doesn't alter my gratitude. I see that the canoe is big enough for me too."

"So it is, Dagaeoga. You can enter it. Take my paddle and work."

The three adjusted their weight in the slender craft, and Robert, taking Willet's paddle instead of Tayoga's, they pushed out into the lake, while the great hunter sat with his long rifle across his knees, watching for the least sign that the warriors might be coming.

CHAPTER II.
THE LIVE CANOE

Robert was fully aware that their peril was not yet over—the Indians, too, might have canoes upon the lake—but he considered that the bulk of it had passed. So his heart was light, and, as they shot out toward the middle of Andiatarocte, he talked of the pursuit and the manner in which he had escaped it.

"I was led the right way by a bird, one that sang," he said. "Your Manitou, Tayoga, sent that bird to save me."

"You don't really believe it came for that special purpose?" asked the hunter.

"Why not?" interrupted the Onondaga. "We do know that miracles are done often. My nation and all the nations of the Hodenosaunee have long known it. If Manitou wishes to stretch out his hand and snatch Dagaeoga from his foes it is not for us to ask his reason why."

Willet was silent. He would not say anything to disturb the belief of Tayoga, he was never one to attack anybody's religion, besides he was not sure that he did not believe, himself.

"We know too," continued Tayoga devoutly, "that Tododaho, the mighty Onondaga chief who went away to his star more than four hundred years ago, and who sits there watching over the Hodenosaunee has intervened more than once in our behalf. He is an arm of Manitou and acts for him."

He looked up. The sky was hidden by the thick darkness. No ray of silver or gray showed anywhere, but the Onondaga knew where lay the star upon which sat his patron saint with the wise snakes, coil on coil, in his hair. He felt that through the banks of mist and vapor Tododaho was watching over him, and, as long as he tried to live the right way taught to him by his fathers, the great Onondaga chieftain would lead him through all perils, even as the bird in brilliant blue plumage had shown Robert the path from the pursuit of Tandakora. The sublime faith of Tayoga never wavered for an instant.

The wind rose a little, a heavy swell stirred the lake and their light craft swayed with vigor, but the two youths were expert canoemen, none better in all the wilderness, and it shipped no water. The hunter, sitting with his hands on his rifle, did not stir, nor did he speak for a long time. Willet, at that moment, shared the faith of his two younger comrades. He was grateful too because once more they had found Robert, for whom he had all the affection of a father. The three reunited were far stronger than the three scattered, and he did not believe that any force on the lakes or in the mountains could trap them. But his questing eyes watched the vast oblong of the lake, looking continually for a sign, whether that of friend or foe.

"What did you find, Robert?" he asked at last.

"Nothing but the band of Tandakora," replied the lad, with a light laugh. "I took my way squarely into trouble, and then I had hard work taking it out again. I don't know what would have happened to me, if you two hadn't come in the canoe."

"It seems," said the Onondaga, in his whimsical precise manner, "that a large part of our lives, Great Bear, is spent in rescuing Dagaeoga. Do you think when we go into the Great Beyond and arrive at the feet of Manitou, and he asks us what we have done with our time on earth, he will put it to our credit when we reply that we consumed at least ten years saving Dagaeoga from his enemies?"

"Yes, Tayoga, we'll get white marks for it, because Robert has also saved us, and there is no nobler work than saving one's fellow creatures. Manitou knows also that it is hard to live in the wilderness and a man must spend a lot of his time escaping death. Look to the east, Tayoga, lad, and tell me if you think that's a point of light on the mountain over there."

The Onondaga studied intently the dark wall of the east, and presently his eyes picked out a dot against its background, infinitesimal like the light of a firefly, but not to be ignored by expert woodsmen.

"Yes, Great Bear," he replied, "I see it is not larger than the littlest star, but it moves from side to side, and I think it is a signal."

"So do I, lad. The lake is narrow here, and the answer, if there be any, will come from the west shore. Now we'll look, all together. Three pairs of eyes are better than one."

The two lads ceased paddling, holding the canoe steady, with an occasional stroke, and began to search the western cliffs in methodical fashion, letting the eye travel from the farthest point in the north gradually toward the south, and neglecting no place in the dark expanse.

"There it is!" exclaimed Robert. "Almost opposite us! I believe it's in the very cliff at the point of which I lay!"

"See it, winking and blinking away."

"Yes, that's it," said Robert. "Now I wonder what those two lights are saying to each other across Lake George?"

"It might be worth one's while to know, for they're surely signaling. It may be about us, or it may be about the army in the south."

"I didn't find anything but trouble," said Robert. "Now what did you and Tayoga find?"

"Plenty traces of both white men and red," replied the hunter. "The forests were full of French and Indians. I think St. Luc with a powerful force is near the north end of Lake George, and the Marquis de Montcalm will soon be at Ticonderoga to meet us."

"But we'll sweep him away when our great army comes up from New York."

"So we should, lad, but the Marquis is an able general, wily and brave. He showed his quality at Fort William Henry and we mustn't underrate him, though I am afraid that's what we'll do; besides the forest fights for the defense."

"It's not like you to be despondent, Dave," said Robert.

"I'm not, lad. I've just a feeling that we should be mighty cautious. Some think the Marquis won't stand when our big army comes, but I do, and I look for a great battle on the shores of either George or Champlain."

"And we'll win it," said Robert in sanguine tones.

"That rests on the knees of the gods," said Willet thoughtfully. "But we've got to deal with one thing at a time. It's our business now to escape from the people who are making those lights wink at each other, or the battle wherever it's fought or whoever wins won't include us because we'll be off on another star, maybe sitting at the feet of Tayoga's Tododaho."

"There's another light on the west shore toward the south," said the Onondaga.

"And a fourth on the eastern cliff also toward the south," added Robert. "All four of them are winking now. It seems to be a general conversation."

"And I wish we could understand their language," said the hunter earnestly. "I'm thinking, however, that they're talking about us. They must have found out in some manner that we're on the lake, and they want to take us."

"Then," said Robert, "it's time for Manitou to send a heavy mist that we may escape in it."

"Manitou can work miracles for those whom he favors," said Tayoga, "and now and then he sends them, but oftenest he withholds his hand, lest we become spoiled and rely upon him when we should rely upon ourselves."

"You never spoke a truer word, Tayoga," said the hunter. "It's the same as saying that heaven helps those who help themselves, and we've got to do a lot of work for ourselves this night. I think the Indian canoes are already on Andiatarocte looking for us."

Robert would have felt a chill had it not been for the presence of his comrades. The danger was unknown, mysterious, it might come from any point, and, while the foe prepared, they must wait until he disclosed himself. Waiting was the hardest thing to do.

"I think we'd better stay just where we are for a while," said the hunter. "It would be foolish to use our strength, until we know what we are using it for. It's certain that Manitou intends to let us fend for ourselves because the night is lightening, which is a hard thing for fugitives."

The clouds floated away toward the north, a star came out, then another, and then a cluster, the lofty shores on either side rose up clear and distinct, no longer vague black walls, the surface of the water turned to gray, but it was still swept by a heavy swell, in which the canoe rocked. Willet finally suggested that they pull to a small island lying on their right, and anchor in the heavy foliage overhanging the water.

"If it grows much lighter they'll be able to see us from the cliffs," he said, "and for us now situated as we are the most important of all things is to hide."

It was a tiny island, not more than a quarter of an acre in size, but it was covered with heavy forest, and they found refuge among the long boughs that touched the water, where they rested in silence, while more stars came out, throwing a silver radiance over the lake. The three were silent and Robert watched the western light that lay farthest south. It seemed to be about two miles away, and, as he looked he saw it grow, until he became convinced that it was no longer a light, but a fire.

"What is the meaning of it?" he asked, calling the attention of Willet.

The hunter looked for a while before replying. The fire still grew and soon a light on the eastern shore began to turn into a fire, increasing in the same manner.

"I take it that they intend to illuminate the lake, at least this portion of it," said Willet. "They'll have gigantic bonfires casting their light far over the water, and they think that we won't be able to hide then."

"Which proves that they are in great force on both shores," said Tayoga.

"How does it prove it?" asked Robert.

The Onondaga laughed softly.

"O Dagaeoga," he said, "you speak before you think. You are always thinking before you speak, but perhaps it is not your fault. Manitou gave you a tongue of gold, and it becomes a man to use that which he can use best. It is very simple. To drag up the fallen wood for such big fires takes many men. Nor would all of them be employed for such work. While some of them feed the flames others are seeking us. We can look for their canoes soon."

"Their plan isn't a bad one for what they want to do," said the hunter. "A master mind must be directing them. I am confirmed in my opinion that St. Luc is there."

"I've been sure of it all the time," said Robert; "it seems that fate intends us to be continually matching our wits against his."

"It's a fact, and it's strange how it's come about," said the hunter thoughtfully.

Robert looked at him, hoping he would say more, but he did not continue the subject. Instead he said:

"That they know what they're doing is shown by the fact that we must move. All the area of the lake about us will be lighted up soon."

The two bonfires were now lofty, blazing pyramids, and a third farther north began also to send its flames toward the sky.

The surface of the lake glowed with red light which crept steadily toward the little island, in the shadow of which the three scouts lay. It became apparent that they had no time to waste, if they intended to avoid being trapped.

"Push out," said Willet, and, with strong sweeps of the paddle, Robert and Tayoga sent the canoe from the shelter of the boughs. But they still kept close to the island and then made for another about a hundred yards south. The glow had not yet come near enough to disclose them, while they were in the open water, but Robert felt intense relief when they drew again into the shelter of trees.

The bonfire on the western shore was the largest, and, despite the distance, he saw passing before the flames tiny black figures which he knew to be warriors or French, if any white men were there. They were still feeding the fire and the pyramid of light rose to an extraordinary height, but Robert knew the peril was elsewhere. It would come on the surface of the lake and he shifted his gaze to the gray waters, searching everywhere for Indian canoes. He believed that they would appear first in the north and he scoured the horizon there from side to side, trying to detect the first black dot when it should show over the lake.

The waters where his eyes searched were wholly in darkness, an unbroken black line of the sky meeting a heaving surface. He looked back and forth over the whole extent, a half dozen times, and found nothing to break the continuity. Hope that the warriors of Tandakora were not coming sprang up in his breast, but he put it down again. Although imagination was so strong in him he was nevertheless, in moments of peril, a realist. Hard experience had taught him long since that when his life was in danger he must face facts.

"There's another island about a half mile away," he said to Willet. "Don't you think we'd better make for it now?"

"In a minute or two, lad, if nothing happens," replied the hunter. "I'd like to see what's coming here, if anything at all comes."

Robert turned his gaze back toward the north, passing his eyes once more to and fro along the line where the dusky sky met the dusky lake, and then he started a little. A dot detached itself from the center of the line, followed quickly by another, another and others. They were points infinitely small, and one at that distance could have told nothing about them from their appearance only, but he knew they were Indian canoes. They could be nothing else. It was certain also that they were seeking the three.

"Do you see them?" asked Robert.

"Yes, and it's a fleet," replied Willet. "They are lighting up the lake with their bonfires, and their canoes are coming south to drive us into the open. There's generalship in this. I think St. Luc is surely in command."

The hunter expressed frank admiration. Often, in the long duel between them and the redoubtable French leader, he paid tribute to the valor and skill of St. Luc. Like Robert, he never felt any hostility toward him. There was nothing small about Willet, and he had abundant esteem for a gallant foe.

"It's time now to run for it again," he said, "and it's important to keep out of their sight."

"I think it will be better for us to swim," said Tayoga, "and let the canoe carry our weapons and ammunition."

"And for us to hide behind it as we've done before. You're right, lad. The canoe is low and does not make much of a blur upon the lake, but if we are sitting upright in it we can be much more easily seen. Now, quick's the word!"

They took off all their outer clothing and moccasins, putting the garments and their weapons into the little craft, and, sinking into the water behind it, pushed out from the overhanging boughs. It was a wise precaution. When they reached the long open stretch of water,

Robert felt that the glow from the nearest bonfire was directly upon them, although he knew that his fancy made the light much stronger than it really was.

The canoe still merged with the color of the waves which were now running freely, and, as the three swam with powerful strokes sending it swiftly ahead of them, Robert was hopeful that they would reach the next island, unseen.

The distance seemed to lengthen and grow interminable, and their pace, although rapid, was to Robert like that of a snail. Yet the longest journey must come to an end. The new island rose at last before them, larger than the others but like the rest covered throughout with heavy forest.

They were almost in its shelter, when a faint cry came from the lofty cliff on the west. It was a low, whining sound, very distant, but singularly penetrating, a sinister note with which Robert was familiar, the Indian war whoop. He recognized it, and understood its significance. Warriors had seen the canoe and knew that it marked the flight of the three.

"What do you think we'd better do?" he said.

"We'll stop for a moment or two at the island and take a look around us," replied Willet.

They moored the canoe, and waded to the shore. Far behind them was the Indian fleet, about twenty canoes, coming in the formation of an arrow, while the bonfires on the cliffs towered toward the sky. A rising wind swept the waves down and they crumbled one after another, as they broke upon the island.

"It looks like a trap with us inside of it," said the hunter. "That shout meant that they've seen our canoe, as you lads know. Warriors have already gone below to head us off, and maybe they've got another fleet, which, answering their signals, will come up from the south, shutting us between two forces."

"We are in their trap," admitted Robert, "but we can break out of it. We've been in traps before, but none of them ever held us."

"So we can, lad. I didn't mean to be discouraging. I was just stating the situation as it now is. We're a long way from being taken."

"The path has been opened to us," said the Onondaga.

"What do you mean?" asked Robert.

"Lo, Dagaeoga, the wind grows strong, and it sweeps toward the south the way we were going."

"I hear, Tayoga, but I don't understand."

"We will send the canoe with wind and waves, but we will stay here."

"Put 'em on a false scent!" exclaimed the hunter. "It's a big risk, but it's the only thing to be done. As the bird saved Robert so the wind may save us! The waves are running pretty fast toward the south now and the canoe will ride 'em like a thing of life. They're too far away to tell whether we are in it."

It was a daring thing to do but Robert too felt that it must be done, and they did not delay in the doing of it. They took out their clothing, weapons, and ammunition, Willet gave the canoe a mighty shove, and it sailed gallantly southward on the crest of the high waves.

"I feel as if I were saying good-by to a faithful friend," said Robert.

"It's more than a friend," said Willet. "It's an ally that will draw the enemy after it, and leave us here in safety."

"If Manitou so wills it," said Tayoga. "It is for him to say whether the men of Tandakora will pass us by. But the canoe is truly alive, Dagaeoga. It skims over the lake like a great bird. If it has a spirit in it, and I do not know that it has not, it guards us, and means to lead away our enemy in pursuit of it."

Quick to receive impressions, Robert also clothed the canoe with life and a soul, a soul wholly friendly to the three, who, now stooping down on the island, amid the foliage, watched the action of the little craft which seemed, in truth, to be guided by reason.

"Now it pauses a little," said Robert. "It's beckoning to the Indian fleet to follow."

"It is because it hangs on the top of a wave that is about to break," said Willet. "Often you see waves hesitate that way just before they crumble."

"I prefer to believe with Dagaeoga," said the Onondaga. "The canoe is our ally, and, knowing that we want the warriors to pass us, it lingers a bit to call them on."

"It may be as you say," said the hunter, "I'm not one to disturb the faith of anybody. If the canoe is alive, as you think, then—it is alive and all the better for us."

"Spirits go into the bodies of inanimate things," persisted the red youth, "and make them alive for a while. All the people of the Hodenosaunee have known that for centuries."

"The canoe hesitates and beckons again," said Robert, "and, as sure as we are here, the skies have turned somewhat darker. The warriors in the fleet or on the shore cannot possibly tell the canoe is empty."

"Again the hand of Manitou is stretched forth to protect us," said Tayoga devoutly. "It is he who sends the protecting veil, and we shall be saved."

"We'll have to wait and see whether the warriors stop and search our island or follow straight after the canoe. Then we'll know," said Willet.

"They will go on," said Tayoga, with great confidence. "Look at the canoe. It is not going so fast now. Why? Because it wishes to tantalize our enemies, to arouse in their minds a belief that they can overtake it. It behaves as if we were in it, and as if we were becoming exhausted by our great exertions with the paddles. Its conduct is just like that of a man who flees for his life. I know, although I cannot see their eyes, that the pursuing warriors think they have us now. They believe that our weakness will grow heavier and heavier upon us until it overpowers us. Tandakora reckons that our scalps are already hanging at his belt. Thus does Manitou make foolish those whom he intends to lead away from their dearest wish."

"I begin to think they're really going to leave us, but it's too early yet to tell definitely," said the hunter. "We shouldn't give them an earthly chance to see us, and, for that reason, we'd better retreat into the heart of the island. We mustn't leave all the work of deception to the canoe."

"The Great Bear is right," said Tayoga. "Manitou will not help those who sit still, relying wholly on him."

They drew back fifteen or twenty yards, and sat down on a hillock, covered with dense bushes, though from their place of hiding they could see the water on all sides. Unless the Indians landed on the island and made a thorough search they would not be found. Meanwhile the canoe was faithful to its trust. The strong wind out of the north carried it on with few moments of hesitation as it poised on breaking waves, its striking similitude to life never being lost for an instant. Robert began to believe with Tayoga that it was, in very fact and truth, alive and endowed with reason. Why not? The Iroquois believed that spirits could go into wood and who was he to argue that white men were right, and red men wrong? His life in the forest had proved to him often that red men were right and white men wrong.

Whoever might be right the canoe was still a tantalizing object to the pursuit. It may have been due to a slight shift of the wind, but it began suddenly to have the appearance of dancing upon the waves, swinging a little to and fro, teetering about, but in the main keeping its general course, straight ahead.

Tayoga laughed softly.

"The canoe is in a frolicsome mood," he said. "It has sport with the men of Tandakora. It dances, and it throws jests at them. It says, 'You think you can catch me, but you cannot. Why do you come so slowly? Why don't you hurry? I am here. See, I wait a little. I do not go as fast as I can, because I wish to give you a better chance.' Ah, here comes the fleet!"

"And here comes our supreme test," said Willet gravely. "If they turn in toward the island then we are lost, and we'll know in five minutes."

Robert's heart missed a beat or two, and then settled back steadily. It was one thing to be captured by the French, and another to be taken by Tandakora. He resolved to fight to the last, rather than fall into the hands of the Ojibway chief who knew no mercy. Neither of the three spoke, not even in whispers, as they watched almost with suspended breath the progress of the fleet. The bonfires had never ceased to rise and expand. For a long distance the surface of the lake was lighted up brilliantly. The crests of the waves near them were tipped with red, as if with blood, and the strong wind moaned like the voice of evil. Robert felt a chill in his blood. He knew that the fate of his comrades and himself hung on a hair.

Nearer came the canoes, and, in the glare of the fires, they saw the occupants distinctly. In the first boat, a large one for those waters, containing six paddles, sat no less a person than the great Ojibway chief himself, bare as usual to the waist and painted in many a hideous design. Gigantic in reality, the gray night and the lurid light of the fires made him look larger, accentuating every wicked feature.

He seemed to Robert to be, in both spirit and body, the prince of darkness himself.

Just behind Tandakora sat two white men whom the three recognized as Auguste de Courcelles and François de Jumonville, the French officers with whom they had been compelled to reckon on other fields of battle and intrigue. There was no longer any doubt that the French were present in this great encircling movement, and Robert was stronger than ever in his belief that St. Luc had the supreme command.

"I could reach Tandakora from here with a bullet," whispered Willet, "and almost I am tempted to do it."

"But the Great Bear will not yield to his temptation," Tayoga whispered back. "There are two reasons. He knows that he could slay Tandakora, but it would mean the death of us all, and the price is too great. Then he remembers that the Ojibway chief is mine. It is for me to settle with him, in the last reckoning."

"Aye, lad, you're right. Either reason is good enough. We'll let him pass, if pass he means, and I hope devoutly that he does."

The fleet preserving its formation was now almost abreast of the island, and once Robert thought it was going to turn in toward them. The long boat of Tandakora wavered and the red giant looked at the island curiously, but, at the last moment the empty canoe, far ahead and dim in the dark, beckoned them on more insistently than ever.

"Now the die is cast," whispered the Onondaga tensely. "In twenty seconds we shall know our fate, and I think the good spirit that has gone into our canoe means to save us."

Tandakora said something to the French officers, and they too looked at the island, but the fleeing canoe danced on the crest of a high wave and its call was potent in the souls of white men and red alike. It was still too far away for them to tell that it was empty. Sudden fear assailed them in the darkness, that it would escape and with it the three who had eluded them so often, and whom they wanted most to take. Tandakora spoke sharply to the paddlers, who bent to their task with increased energy. The long canoe leaped forward, and with it the others.

"Manitou has stretched forth his hand once more, and he has stretched it between our enemies and us," said Tayoga, in a voice of deep emotion.

"It's so, lad," said the hunter, his own voice shaking a little. "I truly believe you're right when you say that as the bird was sent to save Robert so a good spirit was put into the canoe to save us all. Who am I and who is anybody to question the religion and beliefs of another man?"

"Nor will I question them," said Robert, with emphasis.

They were stalwart men in the Indian fleet, skilled and enduring with the paddle, and the fugitive canoe danced before them, a will o' the wisp that they must pursue without rest. Their own canoes leaped forward, and, as the arrow into which they were formed shot past the island, the three hidden in its heart drew the deep, long breaths of those who have suddenly passed from death to life.

"We won't stop 'em!" said Robert in a whimsical tone. "Speed ye, Tandakora, speed ye! Speed ye, De Courcelles and De Jumonville of treacherous memory! If you don't hasten, the flying canoe will yet escape you! More power to your arms, O ye paddlers! Bend to your strokes! The canoe that you pursue is light and it is carried in the heart of the wind! You have no time to lose, white men and red, if you would reach the precious prize! The faster you go the better you will like it! And the better we will, too! On! swift canoes, on!"

"The imagination of Dagaeoga has been kindled again," said Tayoga, "and the bird with a golden note has gone into his throat. Now he can talk, and talk much, without ever feeling weariness—as is his custom."

"At least I have something to talk about," laughed Robert. "I was never before so glad to see the backs of anybody, as I am now to look at the backs of those Indians and Frenchmen."

"We won't do anything to stop 'em," said the hunter.

From their hillock they saw the fleet sweep on at a great rate toward the south, while the fires in the north, no longer necessary to the Indian plan, began to die. The red tint on the water then faded, and the surface of the lake became a solemn gray.

"It's well for us those fires sank," said the hunter, "because while Tandakora has gone on we can't live all the rest of our lives on this little island. We've got to get to the mainland somehow without being seen."

"And darkness is our best friend," said Robert.

"So it is, and in their pursuit of the canoe our foes are likely to relax their vigilance on this part of the lake. Can you see our little boat now, Robert?"

"Just faintly, and I think it's a last glimpse. I hope the wind behind it will stay so strong that Tandakora will never overtake it. I should hate to think that a canoe that has been such a friend to us has been compelled to serve our enemies. There it goes, leading straight ahead, and now it's gone! Farewell, brave and loyal canoe! Now what do you intend to do, Dave?"

"Swim to the mainland as soon as those fires sink a little more. We have got to decide when the head of a swimming man won't show to chance warriors in the bushes, and then make a dash for it, because, if Tandakora overtakes the canoe, he'll be coming back."

"In a quarter of an hour it will be dark enough for us to risk it," said the Onondaga.

Again came the thick dusk so necessary to those who flee for life. Two fires on the high cliffs blazed far in the south, but the light from them did not reach the island where the three lay, where peril had grazed them before going on. The water all about them and the nearer shores lay in shadow.

"The time to go has come," said the hunter. "We'll swim to the western side and climb through that dip between the high cliffs."

"How far would you say it is?" asked Robert.

"About a half mile."

"Quite a swim even for as good swimmers as we are, when you consider we have to carry our equipment. Why not launch one of those fallen trees that lie near the water's edge and make it carry us?"

"A good idea, Robert! A happy thought does come now and then into that young head of yours."

"Dagaeoga is wiser than he looks," said the Onondaga.

"I wish I could say the same for you, Tayoga," retorted young Lennox.

"Oh, you'll both learn," laughed Willet.

As in the ancient wood everywhere, there were fallen trees on the island and they rolled a small one about six inches through at the stem into the lake. They chose it because it had not been down long and yet had many living branches, some with young leaves on them.

"There is enough foliage left to hide our heads and shoulders," said Willet. "The tree will serve a double purpose. It's our ship and also our refuge."

They took off all their clothing and fastened it and the arms, ammunition and knapsacks of food on the tree. Then, they pushed off, with a caution from the hunter that they must not allow their improvised raft to turn in the water, as the wetting of the ammunition could easily prove fatal.

With a prayer that fortune which had favored them so much thus far would still prove kind, they struck out.

CHAPTER III.
IN THE CLIFF

It was only a half mile to the promised land and Robert expected a quick and easy voyage, as they were powerful swimmers and could push the tree before them without trouble.

"When I reach the shore and get well back of the lake," he said to Tayoga, "I mean to lie down in a thicket and sleep forty-eight hours. I am entitled now to a rest that long."

"Dagaeoga will sleep when the spirits of earth and air decree it, and not before," replied the Onondaga gravely. "Can you see anything of our foes in the south?"

"Not a trace."

"Then your eyes are not as good as mine or you do not use them as well, because I see a speck on the water blacker than the surface of the lake, and it is moving."

"Where, Tayoga?"

"Look toward the eastern shore, where the cliff rises tall and almost straight."

"Ah, I see it now. It is a canoe, and it is moving."

"So it is, Dagaeoga, and it is coming our way. Did I not tell you that Manitou, no matter how much he favors us, will not help us all the time? Not even the great and pious Tododaho, when he was on earth, expected so much. Now I think that after saving you with the bird and all of us with the empty canoe he means to leave us to our own strength and courage, and see what we will do."

"And it will be strange, if after being protected so far by a power greater than our own we can't protect ourselves now," said Willet gravely.

"The canoe is coming fast," said Tayoga. "I can see it growing on the water."

"So it is, and I infer from its speed that it has at least four paddles in it. There's no doubt they are disappointed in not finding us farther down, and their boat has come back to look for us."

"This is not the only tree uprooted by the wind and afloat on the lake," said Tayoga, "and now it must be our purpose to make the warriors think it has come into the water naturally."

Long before the French word "camouflage" was brought into general use by a titanic war the art of concealment and illusion was practiced universally by the natives of the North American wilderness. It was in truth their favorite stratagem in their unending wars, and there was high praise for those who could use it best.

"Well spoken, Tayoga," said Willet. "Luckily these living branches hide us, and, as the wind still blows strongly toward the south, we must let the tree float in that direction."

"And not go toward the mainland!" said Robert.

"Aye, lad, for the present. It's stern necessity. If the warriors in that canoe saw the tree floating against the wind they'd know we're here. Trust 'em for that. I think we're about to run another gauntlet."

The trunk now drifted with the wind, though the three edged it ever so slightly, but steadily, toward the shore.

Meanwhile the canoe grew and grew, and they saw, as Willet had surmised, that it contained four paddles. It was evident too that they were on a quest, as the boat began to veer about, and the four Indians swept the lake with eager eyes.

The tree drifted on. Farther to the west and near the shore, another tree was floating in the same manner, and off to the east a third was beckoning in like fashion. There was nothing in the behavior of the three trees to indicate that one of them was different from the other two.

The eyes of the savages passed over them, one after another, but they saw no human being hidden within their boughs. Yet Robert at least, when those four pairs of eyes rested on his tree, felt them burning into his back. It was a positive relief, when they moved on and began to hunt elsewhere.

"They will yet bring their canoe much closer," whispered Willet. "It's too much to expect that they will let us go so easily, and we've got to keep up the illusion quite a while longer. Don't push on the tree. The wind is dying a little, and our pace must be absolutely the pace of the breeze. They notice everything and if we were to go too fast they'd be sure to see it."

They no longer sought to control their floating support, and, as the wind suddenly sank very much, it hung lazily on the crests of little waves.

It was a hard test to endure, while the canoe with the four relentless warriors in it rowed about seeking them. Robert paid all the price of a vivid and extremely brilliant imagination. While those with such a temperament look far ahead and have a vision of triumphs to come out of the distant future, they also see far more clearly the troubles and dangers that confront them. So their nerves are much more severely tried than are those of the ordinary and apathetic. Great will power must come to their relief, and thus it was with Robert. His body quivered, though not with the cold of the water, but his soul was steady.

Although the wind sank, which was against them, the darkness increased, and the fact that two other trees were afloat within view, was greatly in their favor. It gave them comrades in that lazy drifting and diverted suspicion.

"If they conclude to make a close examination of our tree, what shall we do?" whispered Robert.

"We'll be at a great disadvantage in the water," the hunter whispered back, "but we'll have to get our rifles loose from their lashings and make a fight of it. I'm hoping it won't come to that."

The canoe approached the tree and then veered away again, as if the warriors were satisfied with its appearance. Certainly a tree more innocent in looks never floated on the waves of Lake George.

The three were masters of illusion and deception, and they did not do a single thing to turn the tree from its natural way of drifting. It obeyed absolutely the touch of the wind and not that of their hands, which rested as lightly as down upon the trunk. Once the wind stopped entirely and the tree had no motion save that of the swell. It wandered idly, a lone derelict upon a solitary lake.

Robert scarcely breathed when the canoe was sent their way. He was wholly unconscious of the water in which he was sunk to the shoulders, but every imaginative nerve was alive to the immense peril.

"If they return and come much nearer we must immerse to the eyes," whispered Willet. "Then they would have to be almost upon us before they saw us. It will make it much harder for us to get at our weapons, but we must take that risk too."

"They have turned," said Robert, "and here they come!"

It looked this time as if the savages had decided to make a close and careful inspection of the tree, bearing directly toward it, and coming so close that Robert could see their fierce, painted faces well and the muscles rising and falling on their powerful arms as they swept their paddles through the water. Now, he prayed that the foliage of the tree would hide them well and he sank his body so deep in the lake that a little water trickled into his mouth, while only the tips of his fingers rested on the trunk. The hunter and the Onondaga were submerged as deeply as he, the upper parts of their faces and their hair blending with the water. When he saw how little they were disclosed in the dusk his confidence returned.

The four savages brought the canoe within thirty feet, but the floating tree kept its secret. Its lazy drift was that of complete innocence and their eyes could not see the dark heads that merged so well with the dark trunk. They gazed for a half minute or so, then brought their canoe about in a half circle and paddled swiftly away toward the second tree.

"Now Tododaho on his star surely put it in their minds to go away," whispered the Onondaga, "and I do not think they will come back again."

"Even so, we can't yet make haste," said the hunter cautiously. "If this tree seems to act wrong they'll see it though at a long distance and come flying down on us."

"The Great Bear is right, as always, but the wind is blowing again, and we can begin to edge in toward the shore."

"So we can. Now we'll push the tree slowly toward the right. All together, but be very gentle. Robert, don't let your enthusiasm run away with you. If we depart much from the course of the wind they'll be after us again no matter how far away they are now."

"They have finished their examination of the second tree," said Tayoga in his precise school English, "and now they are going to the third, which will take them a yet greater distance from us."

"So they are. Fortune is with us."

They no longer felt it necessary to keep submerged to the mouth, but drew themselves up, resting their elbows on the trunk, floating easily in the buoyant water. They had carefully avoided turning the tree in any manner, and their arms, ammunition and packs were dry and safe. But they had been submerged so long that they were growing cold, and now that the immediate danger seemed to have been passed they realized it.

"I like Lake George," said Robert. "It's a glorious lake, a beautiful lake, a majestic lake, the finest lake I know; but that is no reason why I should want to live in its waters."

"Dagaeoga is never satisfied," said Tayoga. "He might have been sunk in some shallow, muddy lake in a flat country, but instead he is put in this noble one with its beautiful cool waters, and the grand mountains are all about him."

"But this is the second time I've been immersed in a very short space, Tayoga, and just now I crave dry land. I can't recall a single hour or a single moment when I ever wanted it more than I do this instant."

"I'm of a mind with you in that matter, Robert," said the hunter, "and if all continues to go as well as it's now going, we'll set foot on it in fifteen minutes. That canoe is close to the third tree, and they've stopped to look at it. I think we can push a little faster toward the land. They can't notice our slant at that distance. Aye, that's right, lads! Now the cliffs are coming much nearer, and they look real friendly. I see a little cove in there where our good tree can land, and it won't be hard for us to find our way up the banks, though they do rise so high. Now, steady! In we go! It's a snug little cove, put here to receive us. Be cautious how you rise out of the water, lads! Those fellows see like owls in the dark, and they'd trace us outlined here against the shore. That's it, Tayoga, you always do the right thing. We'll crawl out of the lake behind this little screen of bushes. Now, have you lads got all your baggage loose from the tree?"

"Yes," replied Robert.

"Then we'll let it go."

"It's been a fine tree, a kind tree," said Robert, "and I've no doubt Tayoga is right when he thinks a good spirit friendly to us has gone into it."

They pushed it off and saw it float again on the lake, borne on by the wind. Then they dried their bodies as well as they could in their haste, and resumed their clothing. The hunter shook his gigantic frame, and he felt the strength pour back into his muscles and veins, when he grasped his rifle. It had been his powerful comrade for many years, and he now stood where he could use it with deadly effect, if the savages should come.

They rested several minutes, before beginning the climb of the cliff, and saw a second and then a third canoe coming out of the south, evidently seeking them.

"They're pretty sure now that we haven't escaped in that direction," said Willet, "and they'll be back in full force, looking for us. We got off the lake just in time."

The cliffs towered over them to a height of nearly two thousand feet, but they began the ascent up a slanting depression that they had seen from the lake, well covered with bushes, and they took it at ease, looking back occasionally to watch the futile hunt of the canoes for them.

"We're not out of their ring yet," said Willet. "They'll be carrying on another search for us on top of the cliffs."

"Don't discourage us, Dave," said Robert. "We feel happy now having escaped one danger, and we won't escape the other until we come to it."

"Perhaps you're right, lad. We'll enjoy our few minutes of safety while we can and the sight of those canoes scurrying around the lake, looking for their lost prey, will help along our merriment."

"That's true," said Robert, "and I think I'll take a glance at them now just to soothe my soul."

They were about three quarters of the way up the cliff, and the three, turning at the same time, gazed down at a great height upon the vast expanse of Lake George. The night had lightened again, a full moon coming out and hosts of stars sparkling in the heavens.

The surface of the lake gleamed in silver and they distinctly saw the canoes cruising about in their search for the three. They also saw far in the south a part of the fleet returning, and Robert breathed a sigh of thankfulness that they had escaped at last from the water.

They turned back to the top, but the white lad felt a sudden faintness and had he not clung tightly to a stout young bush he would have gone crashing down the slope. He quickly recovered himself and sought to hide his momentary weakness, but the hunter had noticed his stumbling step and gave him a keen, questing glance. Then he too stopped.

"We've climbed enough," he said. "Robert, you've come to the end of your rope, for the present. It's a wonder your strength didn't give out long ago, after all you've been through."

"Oh, I can go on! I'm not tired at all!" exclaimed the youth valiantly.

"The Great Bear tells the truth, Dagaeoga," said the Onondaga, looking at him with sympathy, "and you cannot hide it from us. We will seek a covert here."

Robert knew that any further effort to conceal his sudden exhaustion would be in vain. The collapse was too complete, but he had nothing to be ashamed of, as he had gone through far more than Willet and Tayoga, and he had reached the limit of human endurance.

"Well, yes, I am tired," he admitted. "But as we're hanging on the side of a cliff about fifteen hundred feet above the water I don't see any nice comfortable inn, with big white beds in it, waiting for us."

"Stay where you are, Dagaeoga," said the Onondaga. "We will not try the summit to-night, but I may find some sort of an alcove in the cliff, a few feet of fairly level space, where we can rest."

Robert sank down by the friendly bush, with his back against a great uplift of stone, while Willet stood on a narrow shelf, supporting himself against a young evergreen. Tayoga disappeared silently upward.

The painful contraction in the chest of the lad grew easier, and black specks that had come before his eyes floated away. He returned to a firm land of reality, but he knew that his strength was not yet sufficient to permit of their going on. Tayoga came back in about ten minutes.

"I have found it," he said in his precise school English. "It is not much, but about three hundred feet from the top of the cliff is a slight hollow that will give support for our bodies. There we may lie down and Dagaeoga can sleep his weariness away."

"Camping securely between our enemies above and our enemies below," said Robert, his vivid imagination leaping up again. "It appeals to me to be so near them and yet well hidden, especially as we've left no trail on this rocky precipice that they can follow."

"It would help me a lot if they were not so close," laughed the hunter. "I don't need your contrasts, Robert, to make me rest. I'd like it better if they were a hundred miles away instead of only a few hundred yards. But lead on, Tayoga, and we'll say what we think of this inn of yours when we see it."

The hollow was not so bad, an indentation in the stone, extending back perhaps three feet, and almost hidden by dwarfed evergreens and climbing vines. It was not visible twenty feet above or below, and it would have escaped any eye less keen than that of the Onondaga.

"You've done well, Tayoga," said Willet. "There are better inns in Albany and New York, but it's a pretty good place to be found in the side of a cliff fifteen hundred feet above the water."

"We'll be snug enough here."

They crawled into the hollow, matted the vines carefully in front of them to guard against a slip or an incautious step, and then the three lay back against the wall, feeling an immense relief. While not so worn as Robert, the bones and muscles of Willet and Tayoga also were calling out for rest.

"I'm glad I'm here," said the hunter, and the others were forced to laugh at his intense earnestness.

Robert sank against the wall of the cliff, and he felt an immense peace. The arching stone over his head, and the dwarfed evergreens pushing themselves up where the least bit of soil was to be found, shut out the view before them, but it was as truly an inn to him at that moment as any he had ever entered. He closed his eyes in content and every nerve and muscle relaxed.

"Since you've shut down your lids, lad, keep 'em down," said the hunter. "Sleep will do you more good now than anything else."

But Robert quickly opened his eyes again.

"No," he said, "I think I'll eat first."

Willet laughed.

"I might have known that you would remember your appetite," he said. "But it's not a bad idea. We'll all have a late supper."

They had venison and cold hominy from their knapsacks, and they ate with sharp appetites.

Then Robert let his lids fall again and in a few minutes was off to slumberland.

"Now you follow him, Tayoga," said Willet, "and I'll watch."

"But remember to awake me for my turn," said the Onondaga.

"You can rely upon me," said the hunter.

The disciplined mind of Tayoga knew how to compel sleep, and on this occasion it was needful for him to exert his will. In an incredibly brief time he was pursuing Robert through the gates of sleep to the blessed land of slumber that lay beyond, and the hunter was left alone on watch.

Willet, despite his long life in the woods, was a man of cultivation and refinement. He knew and liked the culture of the cities in its highest sense. His youth had not been spent in the North American wilderness. He had tasted the life of London and Paris, and long use and practice had not blunted his mind to the extraordinary contrasts between forest and town.

He appreciated now to the full their singular situation, practically hanging on the side of a mighty cliff, with cruel enemies seeking them below and equally cruel enemies waiting for them above.

The crevice in which they lay was little more than a dent in the stone wall. If either of the lads moved a foot and the evergreens failed to hold him he would go spinning a quarter of a mile straight down to the lake. The hunter looked anxiously in the dusk at the slender barrier, but he judged that it would be sufficient to stop any unconscious movement. Then he glanced at Robert and Tayoga and he was reassured. They were so tired and sleep had claimed them so completely that they lay like the dead. Neither stirred a particle, but in the silence the hunter heard their regular breathing.

The years had not made Willet a skeptic. While he did not accept unquestioningly all the beliefs of Tayoga, neither did he wholly reject them. It might well be true that earth, air, trees and other objects were inhabited by spirits good or bad. At least it was a pleasing belief and he had no proof that it was not true. Certainly, it seemed as if some great protection had been given to his comrades and himself in the last day or two. He looked up through the evergreen veil at the peaceful stars, and gave thanks and gratitude.

The night continued to lighten. New constellations swam into the heavenly blue, and the surface of the lake as far as eye could range was a waving mass of molten silver. The portion of the Indian fleet that had come back from the south was passing. It was almost precisely opposite the covert now and not more than three hundred yards from the base of the cliff. The light was so good that Willet distinctly saw the paddlers at work and the other warriors sitting upright. It was not possible to read eyes at such a distance, but he imagined what they expressed and the thought pleased him. As Robert had predicted, the snugness of their hiding place with savages above and savages below heightened his feeling of comfort and safety. He was in sight and yet unseen. They would never think of the three hanging there in the side of the cliff. He laughed softly, under his breath, and he had never laughed with more satisfaction.

He tried to pick out Tandakora, judging that his immense size would disclose him, but the chief was not there. Evidently he was with the other part of the fleet and was continuing the vain search in the south. He laughed again and with the same satisfaction when he thought of the Ojibway's rage because the hated three had slipped once more through his fingers.

"An Ojibway has no business here in the province of New York, anyway," he murmured. "His place is out by the Great Lakes."

The canoes passed on, and, after a while, nothing was to be seen on the waves of Lake George. Even the drifting trees, including the one that had served them so well, had gone out of sight. The lake only expressed peace. It was as it might have been in the dawn of time with the passings of no human beings to vex its surface.

Something stirred in the bushes near the hunter. An eagle, with great spread of wing, rose from a nest and sailed far out over the silvery waters. Willet surmised that the nearness of the three had disturbed it, and he was sorry. He had a kindly feeling toward birds and beasts just then, and he did not wish to drive even an eagle from his home. He hoped that it would come back, and, after a while, it did so, settling upon its nest, which could not have been more than fifty yards away, where its mate had remained unmoving while the other went abroad to hunt.

There was no further sign of life from the people of the wilderness, and Willet sat silent a long time. Dawn came, intense and brilliant. He had hoped the day would be cloudy, and he would have welcomed rain, despite its discomfort, but the sun was in its greatest splendor, and the air was absolutely translucent. The lake and the mountains sprang out, sharp and clear. Far to the south the hunter saw a smudge upon the water which he knew to be Indian canoes. They were miles away, but it was evident that the French and Indians still held the lake, and there was no escape for the three by water. There had been some idea in Willet's mind of returning along the foot of the cliffs to their own little boat, but the brilliant day and the Indian presence compelled him to put it away.

The sun, huge, red and scintillating, swung clear of the mighty mountains, and the waters that had been silver in the first morning light turned to burning gold. In the shining day far came near and objects close by grew to twice their size. To attempt to pass the warriors in such a light would be like walking on an open plain, thought the hunter, and, always quick to decide, he took his resolution.

It was characteristic of David Willet that no matter what the situation he always made the best of it. His mind was a remarkable mingling of vigor, penetration and adaptability. If one had to wait, well, one had to wait and there was nothing else in it. He sank down in the little cove in the cliff and rested his back against the stony wall. He, Robert and Tayoga filled it, and his moccasined feet touched the dwarfed shrubs which made the thin green curtain before the opening. He realized more fully now in the intense light of a brilliant day what a slender shelf it was. Any one of them might have pitched from it to a sure death below. He was glad that the white lad and the red lad had been so tired that they lay like the dead. Their positions were exactly the same as when they sank to sleep. They had not stirred an inch in the night, and there was no sign now that they intended to awake any time soon. If they had gone to the land of dreams, they were finding it a pleasant country and they were in no hurry to return from it.

The giant hunter smiled. He had promised the Onondaga to awaken him at dawn, and he knew that Robert expected as much, but he would not keep his promise. He would let nature hold sway; when it chose to awaken them it could, and meanwhile he would do nothing. He moved just a little to make himself more comfortable and reclined patiently.

Willet was intensely grateful for the little curtain of evergreens. Without it the sharp eyes of the warriors could detect them even in the side of the lofty cliff. Only a few bushes stood between them and torture and death, but they stood there just the same. Time passed slowly, and the morning remained as brilliant as ever. He paid little attention to what was passing on the lake, but he listened with all the power of his hearing for anything that might happen on the cliff above them. He knew that the warriors were far from giving up the chase, and he expected a sign there. About two hours after sunrise it came. He heard the cry of a wolf, and then a like cry replying, but he knew that the sounds came from the throats of warriors. He pressed himself a little harder against the stony wall, and looked at his two young comrades. Their souls still wandered in the pleasant land of dreams and their bodies took no interest in what was occurring here. They did not stir.

In four or five minutes the two cries were repeated much nearer and the hunter fairly concentrated all his powers into the organ of hearing. Faint voices, only whispers, floated down to him, and he knew that the warriors were ranging along the cliff just above them. Leaning forward cautiously, he peeped above the veil of evergreens, and saw two dark faces gazing over the edge of the precipice. A brief look was enough, then he drew back and waited.

CHAPTER IV.
THE DARING ATTEMPT

Willet knew from their paint that the faces looking down were those of Huron warriors, but he was quite sure they had not seen anything, and that the men would soon pass on. It was impossible even for the sharpest eyes to pick out the three behind the evergreen screen. Nevertheless he put his rifle forward, ready for an instant shot, if needed, but remained absolutely still, waiting for them to make the next move.

His sensitive hearing brought down the faint voices again and once or twice the light crush of footsteps. Evidently, the warriors were moving slowly along the edge of the cliff, talking as they went, and the hunter surmised that the three were the subject of their attention. He imagined their chagrin at the way in which the chase had vanished, and he laughed softly to think that he and the lads lay so near their enemies, but invisible and so well hidden.

The voices became fainter and died away, the soft crush of footsteps came no more, and the world returned to all the seeming of peace, without any trace of cruelty in it; but Willet was not lured by such an easy promise into any rash act. He knew the savages would come again, and that unbroken vigilance was the price of life. Once more he settled himself into the easiest position and watched. He had all the patience of the Indians themselves, to whom time mattered little, and since sitting there was the best thing to be done he was content to sit there.

Robert and Tayoga slept on. The morning was far gone, but they still rambled happily in the land of dreams, and showed no signs of a wish to return to earth. Willet thought it better that they should sleep on, because youthful bodies demanded it, and because the delay which would be hard for Robert especially would thus pass more easily. He was willing for them to stay longer in the far, happy land that they were visiting.

The sun slowly climbed the eastern arch of the heavens. The day lost none of its intense, vivid quality. The waters of the lake glowed in wonderful changing colors, now gold, now silver, and then purple or blue. Willet even in those hours of anxiety did not forget to steep his soul in the beauty of Lake George. His life was cast amid great and continuous dangers, and he had no family that he could call his own. Yet he had those whom he loved, and if he were to choose over again the land in which to live he would choose this very majestic land in which he now sat. As human life went, the great hunter was happy.

The sound of a shot, and then of a second, came from the cliff above. He heard no cry following them, no note of the war whoop, and, thinking it over, he concluded that the shots were fired by Indians hunting. Since the war, game about the lake had increased greatly, and the warriors, whether attached to the French army or roving at their own will, relied chiefly upon the forest for food. But the reports were significant. The Indian ring about them was not broken, and he measured their own supplies of venison and hominy.

A little after noon Tayoga awoke, and he awoke in the Indian fashion, without the noise of incautious movements or sudden words, but stepping at once from complete sleep to complete consciousness. Every faculty in him was alive.

"I have slept long, Great Bear, and it is late," he said.

"But not too late, Tayoga. There's nothing for us to do."

"Then the warriors are still above!"

"I heard two shots a little while ago. I think they came from hunters."

"It is almost certainly so, Great Bear, since there is nothing in this region for them to shoot at save ourselves, and no bullets have landed near us."

"Yours has been a peaceful sleep. Robert too is now coming out of his great slumber."

The white lad stirred and murmured a little as he awoke. His reentry into the world of fact was not quite as frictionless as that of his Indian comrade.

"Do not fall down the cliff while you stretch yourself, Dagaeoga," said the Onondaga.

"I won't, Tayoga. I've no wish to reach the lake in such fashion. I see by the sun that it's late. What happened while I slept?"

"Two great attacks by Tandakora and his men were beaten off by the Great Bear and myself. As we felt ourselves a match for them we did not consider it necessary to awaken you."

"But of course if you had been pushed a bit harder you would have called upon me. I'm glad you've concluded to use me for tipping the scales of a doubtful combat. To enter at the most strenuous moment is what I'm fitted for best."

"And if your weapons are not sufficient, Dagaeoga, you can make a speech to them and talk them to death."

The hunter smiled. He hoped the boys would always be willing to jest with each other in this manner. It was good to have high spirits in a crisis.

"Take a little venison and hominy, lads," he said, "because I think we're going to spend some time in this most spacious and hospitable inn of ours."

They ate and then were thirsty, but they had no water, although it floated peacefully in millions of gallons below.

"We're dry, but I think we're going to be much dryer," said Willet.

"We must go down one by one in the night for water," said Tayoga.

"We are to reckon on a long stay, then!" said Robert.

"Yes," said Willet, "and we might as well make ourselves at home. It's a great climb down, but we'll have to do it."

"If I could get up and walk about it would be easier," said Robert. "I think my muscles are growing a bit stiff from disuse."

"The descent for water to-night will loosen them up," said Willet philosophically.

It was a tremendously long afternoon, one of the longest that Robert ever spent, and his position grew cramped and difficult. He found some relief now and then in stretching his muscles, but there was nothing to assuage the intense thirst that assailed all three.

Robert's throat and mouth were dry and burning, and he looked longingly at the lake that shimmered and gleamed below them. The waters, sparkling in their brilliant and changing colors, were cool and inviting. They bade him come, and his throat grew hotter and hotter, but he would make no complaint. He must endure it in silence all the afternoon, and all the next day too, if they should be held there.

Late in the afternoon they heard shots again, but they were quite sure that the reports, as before, were due to Indian hunters. Rogers with rangers might be somewhere in the region of the lakes, but they did not think he was anywhere near them. If a skirmish was occurring on the cliff they would hear the shouts of the combatants.

"The warriors will have a feast to-night," said Tayoga.

"And they will have plenty of water to drink," said Robert ruefully. "You remember that time when we were on the peak, and we found the spring in the slope?"

"But there is no spring here," said Tayoga. "We know that because we came up the cliff. There is no water for us this side of the lake."

The afternoon, long as it was, ended at last. The intense burning sunlight faded, and the cool, grateful shadows came. The three stirred in the niche, and Robert felt a little relief. But his throat and mouth were still dry and hard, and they pained him whenever he talked. Yet they forced themselves to eat a scant supper, although the food increased their thirst, but they knew that without it their strength would decrease, and they expected to obtain water in the dark.

The twilight passed, night came, but they waited with infinite patience refusing to move too soon, despite their great thirst. Instead, Tayoga suggested that he go to the crest of the cliff and see if there was a possible way out for them in that direction. Willet agreed, and the Onondaga crept up, without sound, disappearing in a few seconds among the short bushes that hung in the face of the cliff.

Tayoga was a trailer of surpassing skill, and he reached the top without rustling a bush or sending a single pebble rolling. Then he peered cautiously over the rim and beheld a great fire burning not more than a hundred yards away. Thirty or forty warriors were sitting around it, eating. He did not see Tandakora among them, but he surmised, that it was an allied band and that the Ojibway was not far off.

The feast that the three had expected was in full progress. The hunt had been successful, and the Indians, with their usual appetites, were enjoying the results. They broiled or roasted great pieces of deer over the coals, and then devoured them to the last shred. But Tayoga saw that while the majority were absorbed in their pleasant task, a half dozen sentinels, their line extending on either side of the camp, kept vigilant watch. It would be impossible for the three to pass there. They would have to go down to the lake for water, and then hide in their niche.

Tayoga was about to turn back from the cliff, when he heard a shout that he knew was full of significance. He understood the meaning of every cry and he translated it at once into a note of triumph. It sounded like the whoop over the taking of a scalp or the capture of a prisoner, and his curiosity was aroused. Something had happened, and he was resolved to see what it was.

Several of the warriors by the fire replied to the whoop, and then it came again, nearer but with exactly the same note, that of triumph. The Onondaga flattened his body against the earth, and drew himself a little higher. In the dusk, his black eyes glowed with interest, but he knew that his curiosity would soon be gratified. Those who had sent forth the cry were swiftly approaching the camp.

Four warriors came through the undergrowth and they were pushing a figure before them. It was that of a man in a bedraggled and torn red uniform, his hands tied behind him, and all the color gone from his face. Powerful as was his self-control, Tayoga uttered a low cry of surprise. It was the young Englishman, Grosvenor, a prisoner of the hostile warriors, and in a most desperate case.

The Onondaga wondered how he had been taken, but whatever the way, he was in the hands of enemies who knew little mercy.

The warriors around the fire uttered a universal yell of triumph when they saw the captain, and many of them ran forward to meet Grosvenor, whirling their tomahawks and knives in his face, and dancing about as if mad with joy. It was a truly ferocious scene, the like of which was witnessed thousands of times in the great North American forests, and Tayoga, softened by long contact with high types of white men, felt pity. The light from the great fire fell directly on Grosvenor's face and showed its pallor. It was evident that he was weary through and through, but he tried to hold himself erect and he did not flinch when the sharp blades flashed close to his face. But Tayoga knew that his feelings had become blunted. Only the trained forest runner could keep steady in the face of such threats.

When they came near the fire, one of the warriors gave Grosvenor a push, and he fell amid cruel laughter. But he struggled to his feet again, stood a few minutes, and then sank down on a little hillock, where his captors left him alone for the present. Tayoga watched him thoughtfully. He knew that his presence in the Indian camp complicated their own situation. Robert would never hear of going away without an attempt at rescue and Tayoga's own good heart moved him to the same course. Yet it would be almost impossible to take the young Englishman from the center of the Indian camp.

Tayoga knew too what grief his news would cause to young Lennox, between whom and Grosvenor a great friendship had been formed. For the matter of that, both the Onondaga and the hunter also were very partial to the Englishman.

The warriors presently untied Grosvenor's hands and gave him some food. The captive ate a little—he had no appetite for more—and then tried to smooth out his hair and his clothing and to make himself more presentable. He also straightened his worn figure, and sat more erect. Tayoga gave silent approval. Here was a man! He might be a prisoner, and be in a most desperate plight, but he would present the best possible face to his foes. It was exactly what an Onondaga or a Mohawk warrior would do, and the young Englishman, though he knew little of the forest, was living up to its traditions.

"If he has to die," reflected Tayoga, "he will die well. If his people hear that he has gone they will have no cause to be ashamed of the way in which he went. Here is the making of a great white warrior."

The Onondaga knew that Robert and Willet were now expecting him back, but his interest in Grosvenor kept him a while longer, watching at the cliff's rim. He thought it likely that Tandakora might come, and he had not long to wait. The huge Ojibway came striding through the bushes and into the circle of the firelight, his body bare as usual save for breech cloth, leggins and moccasins, and painted with the hideous devices so dear to the savage heart.

The warriors received him with deference, indicating clearly to Tayoga that they were under his authority, but without making any reply to their salutation he strode up to the prisoner, and, folding his arms across his mighty breast, regarded him, smiling cruelly. The Onondaga did not see the smile, but he knew it was there. The man would not be Tandakora if it were not. In that savage heart, the chivalry that so often marked the Indians of the higher type found no place.

Grosvenor, worn to the bone and dazed by the extraordinary and fearful situation in which he found himself, nevertheless straightened up anew, and gave back defiantly the stare of the gigantic and sinister figure that confronted him. Then Tayoga saw Tandakora raise his hand and strike the young Englishman a heavy blow in the face. Grosvenor fell, but sprang up instantly and rushed at the Ojibway, only to find himself before the point of a knife.

The young officer stood still a few minutes, then turned with dignity and sat down once more. Tayoga knew and appreciated his feelings. He had suffered exactly the same humiliation from Tandakora himself, and he meant, with all his soul, that some day the debt should be paid in full. Now in a vicarious way he took upon himself Grosvenor's debt also. The prisoner did not have experience in the woods, his great merits lay elsewhere, but he was the friend of Robert, therefore of Tayoga, and the Onondaga felt it only right that he should pay for both.

Tandakora sat down, a warrior handed him a huge piece of deer meat, and he began to eat. All the others, interrupted for a few minutes by the arrival of the chief, resumed the same pleasant occupation. Tayoga deciding that he had seen enough, began to climb down with great care. The descent was harder than the ascent, but he reached the niche, without noise, and the sight of him was very welcome to Robert and the hunter who had begun to worry over his absence, which was much longer than they had expected.

"Did you see the warriors, Tayoga?" asked young Lennox.

"I saw them, Dagaeoga. They are at the top of the cliff, only two or three hundred yards away; they have a good fire, and they are eating the game they killed in the day."

"And there is no chance for us to pass?"

"None to-night, Dagaeoga. Nor would we pass if we could."

"Why not? I see no reason for our staying here save that we have to do it."

"One is there, Dagaeoga, whom we cannot leave a prisoner in their hands."

"Who? It's not Black Rifle! Nor Rogers, the ranger! They would never let themselves be taken!"

"No, Dagaeoga, it is neither of those. But while I watched at the cliff's rim I saw the warriors bring in that young Englishman, Grosvenor, whom you know and like so well."

"What! Grosvenor! What could he have been doing in this forest!"

"That, I know not, Dagaeoga, save that he has been getting himself captured; how, I know not either, but I saw him brought in a prisoner. Tandakora came, while I watched, and smote the captive heavily in the face with his hand. That debt I take upon myself, in addition to my own."

"You will pay both, Tayoga, and with interest," said the hunter with conviction. "But you were right when you assumed that we could not go away and leave Grosvenor a prisoner in their hands. Because we're here, and because you saw him, your Manitou has laid upon us the duty of saving him."

Robert's face glowed in the dusk.

"We're bound to see it that way," he said. "We'd be disgraced forever with ourselves, if we went away and left him. Now, how are we to do it?"

"I don't know how yet," replied the Onondaga, "but we must first go down to the water. We've forgotten our thirst in the news I bring, but it will soon be on us again, fiercer and more burning than ever. And we must have all our strength for the great task before us."

"I think it's better for all three of us to go down to the lake at once," said Willet. "If anything happens we'll be together, and we are stronger against danger, united than separated. I'll lead the way."

It was a long and slow descent, every step taken with minute care, and as they approached the lake Robert found that his thirst was up and leaping.

"I feel that I could drink the whole lake dry," he said.

"Do not do that, Dagaeoga," said Tayoga in his precise way. "Lake George is too beautiful to be lost."

"We might swim across it," said Willet, looking at the silvery surface of the water unbroken by the dark line of any canoe. "A way has opened to us here, but we can't follow it now."

Robert knelt at the margin, and took a little drink first, letting the cool water moisten his mouth and throat before he swallowed it. How grateful it was! How wonderfully refreshing! One must almost perish with thirst before he knew the enormous value of water. And when it was found, one must know how to drink it right. He took a second and somewhat larger drink. Then, waiting a while, he drank freely and as much as he wanted. Strength, courage, optimism flowed back into his veins. As they came down the cliff he had not seen any way to rescue Grosvenor, nor did he see it now, but he knew that they would do it. His restored body and mind would not admit the possibility of failure.

They remained nearly an hour in the shadow of the bushes at the water's edge, and then began the slow and painful ascent to the niche, which they reached without mishap. Another half hour there, and, having examined well their arms, they climbed to the cliff's rim, where they looked over, and Robert obtained his first view of the Indian camp.

The feasting was over, the fires had sunk far down, and most of the warriors were asleep, but Tandakora himself sat with his arms across his chest, glowering into the coals, and a line of sentinels was set. A red gleam from his uniform showed where Grosvenor, leaning against a log, had fallen at last into a happy slumber, in which his desperate case was forgotten for the time.

"I confess that I don't know how to do it, still it must be done," whispered the hunter.

"Yes, it must be done," the Onondaga whispered back. "We must steal our friend out of the hands of his enemies. Neither do I know how to do it, but perhaps Tododaho will tell me. See, there is his star!"

He pointed to a great star dancing in the sky, a star with a light mist across its face, which he knew to be the wise snakes that lay coil on coil in the hair of the Onondaga sage who had gone away four hundred years ago to his place in the heavens, and prayed for a thought, a happy thought that would tell him the way. In a moment, his mind was in a state of high spiritual exaltation. An electric current seemed to pass from the remote star to him. He shut his eyes, and his face became rapt. In a few minutes, he opened them again and said quietly:

"I think, Great Bear, that Tododaho has told us how to proceed. You and Dagaeoga must draw off the warriors, and then I will take Red Coat from those that may be left behind."

"It's mighty risky."

"Since when, Great Bear, have we been turned aside by risks! Besides, there is no other way."

"It seems that I can't think of any other."

Tayoga unfolded his plan. Robert and Willet must steal along the edge of the cliff and seek to pass to the north of the line of sentinels. If not detected, they would purposely cause an alarm, and, as a consequence, draw off the main portion of the band. Then it was their duty to see to it that they were not taken. Meanwhile Tayoga in the excitement and confusion was to secure the release of Grosvenor, and they would flee southward to the mouth of a small creek, in the lake, where Robert and Willet, after making a great turn, were to join them.

"It's complicated and it's a desperate chance," said Willet thoughtfully, "but I don't see anything else to do. Besides, we have got to act quickly. Being on the war-path, they won't hold him long, and you know the kind of death Tandakora will serve out to him."

Robert shuddered. He knew too well, and knowing so well he was ready to risk his life to save his friend.

"I think," said Tayoga, "that we had better wait until it is about two hours after midnight. Then the minds and bodies of the warriors will be at their dullest, and we will have the best chance."

"Right, Tayoga," said the hunter. "We'll have to use every trifle that's in our favor. Can you see Tandakora from here?"

"He is leaning against the big tree, asleep."

"I'm glad of that. He may be a bit confused when he awakes suddenly and rushes off after us, full tilt, with nearly all the warriors. If only two guards are left with the prisoner, Tayoga, you can dispose of 'em."

"Fortune may favor us."

"Provided we use our wits and strength to the utmost."

"That provision must always be made, Great Bear."

Using what patience they could, they remained at the edge of the cliff, crouched there, until they judged it was about two o'clock in the morning, the night being then at its darkest. Tandakora still slept against his tree, and the fires were almost out. The red gleam from the uniform of Grosvenor could no longer be seen, but Robert had marked well the place where he sat, and he knew that the young Englishman was there, sleeping the sleep of utter exhaustion. Everything was still and peaceful.

"After all, we could escape through their lines, now," whispered Robert.

"So it turns out," said the hunter.

"But it looks as if we were held back in order that we might save Grosvenor."

"That too may be true."

"It is time to go," said Tayoga. "Farewell, Great Bear! Farewell, Dagaeoga! May we meet at the mouth of the creek as we have planned, and may we be four who meet there and not three!"

"May all the stars fight for us," said Robert with emotion, and then he and Willet moved away among the bushes, leaving Tayoga alone at the cliff's rim. Young Lennox knew that theirs was a most perilous venture. Had he given himself time to think about it he would have seen that the chances were about ten to one against its success, but he resolutely closed his mind against that phase of it and insisted upon hope. His was the spirit that leads to success in the face of overwhelming odds.

Willet was first, and Robert was close behind.

Neither looked back, but they knew that Tayoga would not move, until the alarm was given, and they could flee away with the pursuit hot upon their heels. Young Lennox saw again that they could now have slipped through the Indian lines, but the thought of deserting Grosvenor never entered his mind. It seemed though as if all the elements of nature were conspiring to facilitate the flight of the hunter and himself. The sentinels, whose dusky figures they were yet able to see, moved sleepily up and down. No dead wood that would break with a snap thrust itself before their feet. The wilderness opened a way for them.

"I think a warrior or two may be watching in the forest to the north of us," whispered Willet, "but we'll go through the line there. See that fellow standing under the tree, about a hundred yards to the south. He's the one to give the alarm."

But circumstances still favored them. Nature was peaceful. When they wished for the first time in their lives that their flight should be detected, nothing happened, and the vigilance of the warriors who usually watched so well seemed to be relaxed. Robert was conscious that they were passing unseen and unheard between the sentinel on the north and the sentinel on the south.

Two hundred yards farther on, and the hunter brought his moccasin sharply down upon a dead stick which broke with a sharp snap, a sound that penetrated far in the still night. Robert, glancing back, saw the sentinel on the south stiffen to attention and then utter a cry of alarm, a shout sufficient to awaken any one of the sleeping Indians. It was given back in an instant by several voices from the camp, and then the hunter and the youth sprang to their task.

"Now we're to run as we've never run before," exclaimed Willet. "But we must let 'em think they're going to catch us."

First, sending back a tremendous shout of defiance that he knew would enrage Tandakora's men to the utmost, he raced with long swift steps through the forest, and Robert was always close on his heels. The yells of the Indians behind them, who pushed forward in pursuit, were succeeded by silence, and Robert knew they now were running for their lives. Luckily, they were coming into a country with which the hunter had some acquaintance, and, turning a little to the south, he led the way into a ravine down which they took a swift course. After a mile or so he stopped, and the two rested their lungs and muscles.

"They can't see our trail to-night," said the hunter, "and they'll have to depend on eye and ear, but they'll stick to the chase for a long time. I've no doubt they think all three of us are here, and that they may take us in one haul. Ready to start on again, Robert?"

"My breath is all right now, and I'll run a race with anybody. You don't think they've lost us, do you?"

"Not likely, but in case they have I'll tell 'em where we are."

He uttered a shout so piercing that it made Robert jump. Then he led again at a great pace down the ravine, and a single cry behind them showed that the pursuit was coming. As nearly as Robert could calculate, the warriors were about three hundred yards away. He could not see them, but he was sure they would hang on as long as the slightest chance was left to overtake Willet and himself.

They fled in silence at least another mile, and then, feeling their breath grow difficult again, they stopped a second time, still in the ravine and among thick bushes.

"Our flight may be a joke on them, as we intend to draw them after us," said Robert, "but constant running turns it into a joke on us too. I've done so much of this sort of thing in the last few days that I feel as if I were spending my life, dodging here and there in the forest, trying to escape warriors."

Willet laughed dryly.

"It's not the sort of life for a growing youth," he said, "but you'll have to live it for a while. Remember our task. If they lose our trail it's our business to make 'em find it again. Here's another challenge to 'em."

He shouted once more, a long, defiant war cry, much like that of the warriors themselves, and then he and Robert resumed their flight, leaving the ravine presently, and taking a sharper course toward the south.

"I think we'd have lost 'em back there if it hadn't been for that whoop of mine," said Willet.

"Perhaps it's about time to lose them," said Robert hopefully. "The sooner we do it the happier I'll feel."

"Not yet, Robert, my lad. We must give Tayoga all the time he needs for the work he's trying to do. After all, his task is the main one, and the most dangerous. I think we can slow up a bit here. We have to save our breath."

They dropped down to a walk, and took another deep curve toward the south, and now also to the east. Their present course, if persisted in, would bring them back to the lake. The night was still dark, but their trained eyes had grown so used to it that they could see very well in the dusk. Both were looking back and at the same time they saw a shadowy figure appear in the forest behind them. Robert knew that it was the vanguard of the pursuit which was drawing uncomfortably close, at least for him. A shout from the warriors was followed by a shot, and a bullet cut its way through the leaves near them.

"I think we ought to give 'em a hint that they come too close, at their peril," said Willet, and raising his own rifle he sent back an answering shot which did not go astray. The first warrior fell, and others who had come forward in the undergrowth gave back for the time.

"They'll take the hint," said the hunter, "and now we'll increase our speed."

He reloaded, as they ran, and a little later Robert sent a bullet that struck the mark. Once more the warriors shrank back for the time, and the hunter and lad, using their utmost speed, fled toward the southwest at such a great rate that the pursuit, at length, was left behind and finally was lost. Day found their foes out of sight, and two or three hours later they came to the mouth of the creek, where they were to meet Tayoga, in case he succeeded.

"And now the rest is in other hands than ours," said Willet.

Forcing themselves to assume a patience they could scarcely feel, they sat down to wait.

CHAPTER V.
TAYOGA'S SKILL

They still had food left in their knapsacks, and they ate a portion, drinking afterward from the creek. Then they resumed their places in the dense undergrowth, where they could watch well and yet remain hidden. They could also see from where they lay the shimmering waters of Andiatarocte, and the lake seemed to be once more at peace. They felt satisfaction that they had completed their part of the great enterprise, but their anxiety nevertheless was intense. As Willet had truly said, Tayoga's share was the more dangerous and delicate by far.

"Do you think he will come?" Robert asked after a long silence.

"If any human being could come under such circumstances and bring Grosvenor with him, it is Tayoga," replied the hunter. "I think sometimes that the Onondaga is superhuman in the forest."

"Then he will come," said Robert hopefully.

"Best not place our hopes too high. The hours alone will tell. It's hard work waiting, but that's our task."

The morning drew on. Another beautiful day had dawned, but Robert scarcely noticed its character. He was thinking with all his soul of Tayoga and Grosvenor. Would they come? Willet was able to read his mind. He was intensely anxious himself, but he knew that the strain of waiting upon Robert, with his youthful and imaginative mind, was greater. He was bound to be suffering cruelly.

"We must give them time," he said. "Remember that Grosvenor is not used to the woods, and can't go through them as fast as we can. We must have confidence too. We both know what a wonder Tayoga is."

Robert sprang suddenly to his feet.

"What was that!" he exclaimed.

A sound had come out of the north, just a breath, but it was not the wind among the leaves, nor yet the distant song of a bird. It was the faint howl of a wolf, and yet Robert believed that it was not a wolf that made it.

"Did you hear it?" he repeated.

"Aye, lad, I heard it," replied the hunter. "'Tis a signal, and 'tis Tayoga too who comes. But whether he comes alone, or with a friend, I know not. To tell that we must bide here and see."

"Should not we send our answer?"

"Nay, lad. He knows where we are. This is the appointed place, and the fewer signals we give the less likely the enemy is to get a hint we're here. I don't think we will hear from Tayoga again until he shows in person."

Robert said no more, knowing full well the truth of the hunter's words, but his heart was beating hard, and he stirred nervously. He had been drawn strongly to Grosvenor, and he knew what a horrible fate awaited him at the hands of Tandakora, unless the Onondaga saved him. Nor would there be another chance for interruption by Tayoga or anybody else. But the minutes passed and he took courage. Tayoga had not yet come. If alone he would have arrived by this time. His slowness must be due to the fact that he had Grosvenor with him. More minutes passed and he heard steps in the undergrowth. Now he was sure. Tayoga was not alone. His moccasins never left any sound. He stood up expectant, and two figures appeared among the bushes. They were Tayoga, calm, his breath unhurried, a faint smile in his dark eyes, and Grosvenor, exhausted, reeling, his clothing worse torn than ever, but the light of hope on his face. Robert uttered a cry of joy and grasped the young Englishman's hand.

"Thank God, you are here!" he exclaimed.

"I thank God and I thank this wonderful young Indian too," panted Grosvenor. "It was a miracle! I had given up hope when he dropped from the skies and saved me!"

"Sit down and get your breath, man," said Willet. "Then you can tell us about it."

Grosvenor sank upon the ground, and did not speak again until the pain in his laboring chest was gone. Tayoga leaned against a tree, and Robert noticed then that he carried an extra rifle and ammunition.

The Onondaga thought of everything. Willet filled his cap with water at the creek, and brought it to Grosvenor, who drank long and deeply.

"Tastes good!" said the hunter, smiling.

"Like nectar," said the Englishman, "but it's nectar to me too to see both of you, Mr. Willet and Mr. Lennox. I don't understand yet how it happened. It's really and truly a miracle."

"A miracle mostly of Tayoga's working," said the hunter.

"I thought the end of everything for me had come," said Grosvenor, "and I was only praying that it might not be harder for me than I could stand, when the alarm was heard in the forest, and nearly all the Indians ran off in pursuit of something or other. Only two were left with me. There was a shot from the woods, one of them fell, this wonderful friend of yours appeared from the forest, wounded the other, who took to his heels, then we started running in the other direction, and here we are. It's a marvel and I don't yet see how it was done."

"Tayoga's marvelous knowledge of the woods, his skill and his quickness made the greater part of the miracle," said the hunter, "and you see too, Lieutenant Grosvenor, that he even had the forethought to bring away with him the rifle and ammunition of the fallen warrior, that you might have arms now that you are strong enough to bear them again."

Tayoga without a word handed him the rifle and ammunition, and Grosvenor felt strength flowing back into his body when he took them.

"Could you eat a bite?" asked Willet.

"I think I could now," replied the Englishman, "although I'll confess I've had no appetite up to the present. My situation didn't permit hunger."

Willet handed him a piece of venison and he ate. Meanwhile Tayoga, who seemed to feel no weariness, and the others were watching. In a short time the hunter announced that it was time to go.

"We can't afford to delay here any longer and have 'em overtake us!" he said. "We're out of the ring now, and it's our affair to keep out. Lieutenant Grosvenor, you can tell us as we go along how you happened to be the prisoner of Tandakora."

"It needs only a few words," said the Englishman as they took their way southward through the woods. "I was at Albany with a body of troops, a vanguard for the force that we mean to march against the French at Ticonderoga. I was sent northward with ten men to scour the country, and in the woods we were set upon suddenly by savage warriors. My troopers were either killed or scattered, and I was taken. That was yesterday morning. Since then I have been hurried through the forest, I know not where, and I have had a most appalling experience. As I have said before, I'd long since given up hope for a miracle like the one that has saved me. What a horrible creature that giant Indian was!"

"Tandakora is all that you think him and more. He's been hunting us too, and when he comes back to his camp he'll be after us all four again. So, that's why we hurry."

"You're in no bigger hurry than I am," said Grosvenor with attempt at a smile. "If I could find the seven-league boots I'd put them on."

Tayoga once more led the way, and he examined the forest on all sides with eyes that saw everything.

Robert and Willet were greatly refreshed by their rest at the creek, and the promise of life that had been made again so wonderfully put new strength in Grosvenor's frame. So they were able to travel at a good pace, though the three listened continually for any sound that might indicate pursuit.

Yet as the morning progressed there was no hostile sign and their confidence rose.

Robert hoped most devoutly that they would soon come within the region of friends. While the French and Indians held the whole length of Lake Champlain and it was believed Montcalm would fortify somewhere near Ticonderoga, yet Lake George was debatable. It was generally considered within the British and American sphere, although they were having ample proof that fierce bands of the enemy roved about it at will.

Aside from the danger there was another reason why he wished so earnestly for escape from this tenacious pursuit. They were seeing the bottoms of their knapsacks. One could not live on air and mountain lakes alone, however splendid they might be, and, although the wilderness usually furnished food to three such capable hunters, they could not seek game while Tandakora and his savage warriors were seeking them. So, their problem was, in a sense, economic, and could not be fought with weapons only.

At a signal from Willet, who observed that Grosvenor was somewhat tired, they sank their pace to a slow walk, and in about three hours stopped entirely, sitting down on fallen timber which had been heaped in a windrow by a passing hurricane. They were still in dense forest and had borne away somewhat from Andiatarocte, but, through the foliage, they caught glimpses of the lake rippling peacefully in silver and blue and purple.

"Once more I want to thank you fellows for saving me," said Grosvenor.

"Don't mention it again," said the hunter. "In the wilderness we have to save one another now and then, or none of us would live. Your turn to rescue us may come before you think."

"I know nothing of the forest. I feel helpless here."

"Just the same, you don't know what weapon Tayoga's Manitou may place in your hands. The border brings strange and unexpected chances. But our present crisis is not over. We're not saved yet, and we can't afford to relax our efforts a particle. What is it, Tayoga?"

The Onondaga, rising from the fallen tree, had gone about twenty yards into the forest, where he was examining the ground, obviously with great concentration of both eye and mind. He waited at least a minute before replying. Then he said:

"Our friend, the lone ranger, Black Rifle, has passed here."

"How can you know that?" asked Grosvenor in surprise.

"Come and look at his traces," said Tayoga. "See where he has written his name in the earth; that is, he has left what you would call in Europe his visiting card."

Grosvenor looked attentively at the ground, but he saw only a very faint impression, and he never would have noticed that had not the Onondaga pointed it out to him.

"It might have been left by a deer," he objected.

"Impossible," said Tayoga. "The entire imprint is not made, but there is enough to indicate very clearly that a human foot and nothing else pressed there. Here is another trace, although lighter, and here another and another. The trail leads southward."

"But granting it to be that of a man," Grosvenor again objected, "it might be that of any one of the thousands who roam the wilderness."

The great red trailer who had inherited the forest lore of countless generations smiled.

"It is not any one of the thousands and it could not be," he said. "It is easy to tell that. The footsteps are those of a white man, because they turn out, and not in, as do ours of the red race. That is very easy; even Dagaeoga here, the great talker, knows it. The footsteps are far apart, so we are sure that they are those of a tall man; the imprints are deep, proving them to have been made by a heavy man, and at the outer edge of the heel the impression is deeper than on the inner edge. I noticed, when we last saw Black Rifle, which was not long ago, that he wore moccasins of moose hide, that he had turned them outward a little, through wear, and that a small strip of the hardest moose hide had been sewed on the right edge of each heel in order to keep them level. Those strips have made their marks here."

"Somebody else might have put strips of hide on his moccasin heels!"

"It is so, but Black Rifle is tall and large and heavy, and we know that the man who made this trail is tall, large and heavy. The chances are a hundred to one against the fact that any other man tall, large and heavy with moose hide strips to even the wear of his moccasin heels has passed here, especially as this is within the range of Black Rifle. I know that it is he as truly as I know that I am standing here."

"Of course," said Robert, who had never felt the slightest doubt of Tayoga's knowledge. "What was Black Rifle doing?"

"He was looking for St. Luc or Tandakora, because his trail does not lead straight on. See! here it comes, and here again. If Black Rifle had been on a journey he would have gone straight, but he is seeking something and so he turns about. Ah, he wishes to see if there are any canoes visible on the lake, for lo! the trail now leads toward the water! Here he found that none was to be seen and here he rested. Black Rifle had been long on his feet, two days and two nights perhaps, because it takes much to make him weary. He sat on this log. He left a strand from the fringe of his buckskin hunting shirt, caught on a splinter. Do you not see it, Lieutenant Grosvenor?"

"Now that you hold it up before my eyes I notice it But I should never have found it in the wilderness." "Minute observation is what every trailer has to learn," said Willet, "else you are no trailer at all, and you'll learn, Lieutenant, while you are with us, that Tayoga is probably the greatest trailer the world has ever produced."

"Peace, Great Bear! Peace!" protested the Onondaga.

"It's so, just the same. Now, what did Black Rifle do after he rested himself on the log?"

"He went back farther into the woods, turning away from the lake," replied Tayoga, "and he sat down again on another fallen log. Black Rifle was hungry, and he ate. Here is the small bone of a deer, picked quite clean, lying on the ground by the log. Black Rifle was a fortunate man. He had bread, too. See, here is a crumb in this crack in the log too deep down for any bird to reach with his bill. Black Rifle sat here quite a long time. He was thinking hard. He did not need so much time for resting. He remained sitting on the log while he was trying to decide what he would do. It is likely that Black Rifle thought a great force was behind him, and he turned back to see. Had he kept straight on toward the south, as he was going at first, he would not have needed so much time for thinking over his plans. Ah, he has turned! Lo! his trail goes almost directly back on his own course. It will lead to the top of the hillock there, because he wants to see far, and I think that after seeing he will turn again, and follow his original course."

"Why do you think that?" asked Grosvenor.

"Because, O Red Coat, it is likely that Black Rifle knew from the first which way he wanted to go and went that way. He has merely turned back, like a wise general, to scout a little, and see that no danger comes from the rear. Yes, he stood here on the hillock from which we can get a good view over the country, and walked to every side of the crest to find where the best view could be obtained. That, Red Coat, is the simplest of all things. Behold the traces of his moccasins as he walked from side to side. Nothing else could have made Black Rifle move about so much in the space of a few square yards. Now he leaves the hillock and goes down its side toward a low valley in which runs a brook. Black Rifle is thirsty and will drink deep."

"That you can't possibly know, Tayoga."

"But I do know it, Red Coat."

"You don't even know a brook is near."

"I know it, because I have seen it. My eyes are trained to the forest, and I caught the gleam of running water through the leaves to the west. Running water, of course, means a brook. Black Rifle's trail now leads toward it, and I assume that he was thirsty because he had just eaten well. We are nearly always thirsty after eating. But we shall see whether I am right. Here is the brook, and there are the faint traces made by Black Rifle's knees, when he knelt to reach the water. He started away, but found that he was still thirsty, so he came back and drank again. Here are his footprints about a yard from the others. This time, he will go back toward the south, and I think it is sure that he is looking for St. Luc, who must have gone in that direction with a strong force, Tandakora having stayed behind to take us. It is likely that Black Rifle went on, because a great British and American army is gathering below, which fact he knows well, and it is probable that Black Rifle follows St. Luc, because he will hunt the biggest game."

Grosvenor's eyes sparkled.

"I understand," he said. "It is a great art, that of trailing through the wilderness, and I can see how circumstances compel you to learn it."

"We have to learn it to live," said the hunter gravely, "but with Tayoga it is an art carried to the highest degree of perfection. He was born with a gift for it, a very great gift. He inherited all the learning accumulated by a thousand years of ancestors, and then he added to it by his own supreme efforts."

"Do not believe all that Great Bear tells you," said Tayoga modestly. "For unknown reasons he is partial to me, and enlarges my small merits."

"I think this would be a good place for all of you to wait, while I went back on the trail a piece," said the hunter. "If Black Rifle found it necessary to cover the rear, it's a much more urgent duty for us who know that we've been followed by Tandakora to do the same."

"The Great Bear is always wise," said Tayoga. "We will take our ease while we await him."

He flung himself down on the turf and relaxed his figure completely. He had learned long since to make the most of every passing minute, and, seeing Robert imitate him exactly, Grosvenor did likewise. The hunter had disappeared already in the bushes and the three lay in silence.

Grosvenor felt an immense peace. Brave as a young lion, he had been overwhelmed nevertheless by his appalling experiences, and his sudden rescue where rescue seemed impossible had taken him back to the heights. Now, it seemed to him that the three, and especially the Onondaga, could do everything. Tayoga's skill as a trailer and scout was so marvelous that no enemy could come anywhere near without his knowledge. The young Englishman felt that he was defended by impassable walls, and he was so free from apprehension that his nerves became absolutely quiet. Then worn nature took its toll, and his eyelids drooped. Before he was aware that he was sleepy he was asleep.

"You might do as Red Coat has done, Dagaeoga," said Tayoga. "I can watch for us all, and it is wise in the forest to take sleep when we can."

"I'll try," said Robert, and he tried so successfully that in a few minutes he too slumbered, with his figure outstretched, and his head on his arm. Tayoga made a circle about three hundred yards in diameter about them, but finding no hostile sign came back and lay on the turf near them. He relaxed his figure again and closed his eyes, which may have seemed strange but which was not so in the case of Tayoga. His hearing was extraordinarily acute, and, when his eyes were shut, it grew much stronger than ever. Now he knew that no warrior could come within rifle shot of them without his ears telling him of the savage approach. Every creeping footstep would be registered upon that delicate drum.

With eyes shut and brain rested, Tayoga nevertheless knew all that was going on near him. That eardrum of infinite delicacy told him that a woodpecker was tapping on a tree, well toward the north; that a little gray bird almost as far to the south was singing with great vigor and sweetness; that a rabbit was hopping about in the undergrowth, curious and yet fearful; that an eagle with a faint whirr of wings had alighted on a bough, and was looking at the three; that the eagle thinking they might be dangerous had unfolded his wings again and was flying away; that a deer passing to the west had caught a whiff of them on the wind and was running with all speed in the other direction; that a lynx had climbed a tree, and, after staring at them, had climbed down again, and had fled, his coward heart filled with terror.

Thus Tayoga, with his ears, watched his world. He too, his eyelids lowered, felt a peace that was soothing and almost dreamy, but, though his body relaxed, those wonderfully sensitive drums of his ears caught and registered everything. The record showed that for nearly two hours the life of the wilderness went on as usual, the ordinary work and play of animal and bird, and then the drums told him that man was coming. A footstep was registered very clearly, and then another and another, but Tayoga did not open his eyes. He knew who was coming as well as if he had seen him. The drums of his ears made signals that his mind recognized at once. He had long known the faint sound of those footsteps. Willet was coming back.

Tayoga, through the faculty of hearing, was aware of much more than the mere fact that the hunter was returning. He knew that Willet had found nothing, that the pursuit was still far away and that they were in no immediate danger. He knew it by his easy, regular walk, free from either haste or lagging delay. He knew it by the straight, direct line he took for the three young men, devoid of any stops or turnings aside to watch and listen. Willet's course was without care.

Tayoga opened his eyes, and lazily regarded the giant figure of his friend now in full view. Robert and Grosvenor slept on. "I am glad," said the Onondaga.

It was significant of the way in which they understood each other and the way they could read the signs of the forest that they could talk almost without words.

"So am I," said the hunter, "but I had hoped for it."

"Since it is so, we need not awaken them just yet."

"No, let them sleep another hour."

Tayoga meant that he was glad the enemy had not approached and Willet replied that he had hoped for such good luck. No further explanation was needed.

"You had the heaviest part of the burden to carry, last night," said the hunter, "so it would be wise for you to join them if you can, in the hour that's left. See if you can't follow them, at once."

"I think I can," said Tayoga. "At least I will try."

In five minutes he too had gone to the land of dreams and the hunter watched alone. Willet, although weary, was in high spirits. They had come marvelously through many perils, and Tayoga's achievement in rescuing Grosvenor, he repeated to himself, was well nigh miraculous. After such startling luck they could not fail, and an omen of continued good fortune was the fact they had encountered the trail of Black Rifle. He would be a powerful addition to their little force, when found, and Willet did not doubt that they would overtake him. The only problem that really worried him now was that of food. Small as was their army of four, it had to be provisioned, and, for the present, he did not see the way to do it.

He let the three sleep overtime, and when they awoke they were grateful to him for it.

"I am quite made over," said Grosvenor, "and I think that if I stay in the wilderness long enough I may learn to be a scout too. But as all my life has been spent in quite different kinds of country, I suppose it will take a hundred years to give me a good start."

Tayoga smiled.

"Not a hundred years," he said. "Red Coat has begun very well."

"And now with a lot of good solid food I'll feel equal to any march," continued Grosvenor. "Most Englishmen, you know, eat well."

Tayoga looked at Robert, who looked at Willet, who in his turn looked at the Onondaga.

"That's just what we'll have to do without," said the hunter gravely. "The bottoms of our knapsacks are looking up at us. We'll have a splendid chance to see how long we can do without food. One needs such a test now and then."

Grosvenor's face fell, but his was the true mettle. In an instant his countenance became cheerful again.

"I'm not hungry!" he exclaimed. "It was the delusion of a moment, and it passed as quickly as it came. I suffer from such brief spells."

The others laughed.

"That's the right spirit," said Willet, "and while we have nothing to eat we have lots of hope. I've been hungrier than this often, and, as you see, I've never starved to death a single time. There's always lots of food somewhere in the wilderness, if you only know how to put your hand on it."

"I think it is now best for us to follow on the trail of Black Rifle," said Tayoga.

"That's so," responded the hunter. "It's grown a lot colder, while you lads slept, though I think you can follow it without any trouble, Tayoga."

The red lad said nothing, but at once picked up the traces, which now led south, slanting back a little toward the lake.

"Black Rifle was going fast," he said. "His stride lengthens. He must have divined where St. Luc with his force lay, and he took a direct course for it. Ah, he turns suddenly aside and walks to and fro."

"That's curious," said the hunter. "I see the footprints all about. What did Black Rifle mean by moving about in such a manner?"

"It is not odd at all," said Tayoga. "Doubtless Black Rifle was suffering from the same lack that we are, and it was necessary for him to provision his army of one at once. He suddenly saw a chance to do so and he turned aside from his direct journey toward the south. So we shall soon see where Black Rifle shot his bear."

"And why not a deer?" said Grosvenor.

"Because his trail now leads toward that deep thicket on our right, a thicket made up of bushes and vines and briars. A deer could not have gone into it, but a bear could, and we know now it was a bear, because here are its tracks. Black Rifle killed the bear in the thicket."

"Are you sure of that, Tayoga?" asked Robert.

"Absolutely sure, Dagaeoga. It is in this case a matter of mind and not of eye. Black Rifle is too good a hunter to fire a useless shot, and too experienced to miss his game, when he needs it so badly. He would take every precaution for success. My mind tells me that it was impossible for him to miss."

"And he didn't miss," said Robert, as they entered the thicket. "See where the vines and briars were threshed about by the bear as he fell. Here are spots of blood, and here goes the path along which he dragged the body. All this is as plain as day."

"It was a fat bear too," said Tayoga. "Although it is early spring he had found so many good roots and berries that he had more than made up for the loss of weight in his long winter fast. We will soon find where Black Rifle cleaned his prize. A bear is too heavy to carry far. Ah, he did his work just beyond us in the little valley!"

"How do you know that?" asked Grosvenor. "We can't yet see into the valley."

The great red trailer smiled.

"This time, O Red Coat," he replied, "it is a combination of mind and eye. Mind tells me that Black Rifle could not clean and dress his bear unless he got it to water. Mind tells me that a brook is flowing in the valley just ahead of us, because there is scarcely a valley in the country that does not have its brook. Eye tells me that Black Rifle finished his task by the great oak there. Do you not see the huge buzzards flying above the tree? They are conclusive. Ah, the forest people gathered fast in numbers! They expected that Black Rifle would leave them a great feast."

They found a little brook of clear, cold water and, beside it, the place where Black Rifle had cleaned his bear, reserving afterward the choice portion for himself.

"When he went on," said Tayoga, "the forest people made a rush for what he did not want, which was much. Great birds came. We cannot see their trail through the air, but we can see where they hopped about here on the ground, tore at the flesh, and fought with one another for the spoil. A lynx came, and then another, and then wolves. The weasel and the mink too hung on the outskirts, waiting for what the bigger animals might leave. Among them they left nothing and they were not long in the task."

Only shining bones lay on the ground. They had been picked clean and all the forest people had gone after their brief banquet. The trails led away in different directions, but that of Black Rifle went on toward the south. The traces, however, were more distinct than they had been before he stopped for the bear.

"It is because he is carrying much weight," said Tayoga. "Black Rifle no longer skips along like a youth, as Red Coat here does."

"You can have all the sport with me you wish," said Grosvenor. "I don't forget that you saved my life, when by all the rules of logic it was lost beyond the hope of recovery."

"Black Rifle would not eat so much bear meat himself," said Tayoga, "nor would he carry such a burden, without good cause. It may be that he expects us. He has perhaps heard that we are in this region."

"It's possible," said the hunter.

Full of eagerness, they pressed forward on the trail.

CHAPTER VI.
BLACK RIFLE

They had been following the trail about half an hour, when Tayoga noticed that it was growing deeper.

"Ah," he said, "Black Rifle now walks much more slowly, so slow that he barely creeps, and his feet press down harder. I think he is going to make another stop."

"Maybe he intends to cook a part of that fat bear," said Grosvenor, struggling hard, though, to keep all trace of envy out of his voice. "You said a while back that he was going to kill the bear, because he was hungry, and it seems to me that he would be a very foolish man, if having got his bear, he didn't make use of any portion of it."

Tayoga laughed with sincere enjoyment.

"Red Coat reasons well," he said. "If a man is eager to eat, and he has that which he can eat, then he would be a silly man if he did not eat. Red Coat has all the makings of a trailer. In a few more yards, Black Rifle will stop and cook himself a splendid dinner. Here he put his bear meat upon this log. The red stains show it. Then he picked up dead and fallen wood, and broke it into the right length over the log. You can see where he broke places in the bark at the same time. Then he heaped them all in the little hollow, where he has left the pile of ashes. But, before he lighted a fire, with his flint and steel, he made a wide circle all about to see if any enemy might be near. We knew he would do that because Black Rifle is a very cautious man, but his trail proves it to any one who wishes to look. Then, satisfied, he came back, and started the flame. But he kept the blaze very low lest a prowling foe see it. When the bed of coals was fanned he cooked large portions of the bear and ate, because Black Rifle was hungry, ah, so hungry! and the bear was very savory and pleasing to his palate!"

"Stop, Tayoga, stop!" exclaimed Grosvenor, "I can't stand such torture! You'll make me starve to death where I stand."

"But as you are about to become a warrior of the woods, Red Coat," said the Onondaga gravely, "you must learn to endure. Among us a warrior will purposely put the fire to his hand or his breast and hold it there until the flesh smokes. Nor will he utter a groan or even wince. And all his people will applaud him and call him brave."

Grosvenor shuddered. He did not see the lurking gleam of humor in the eye of Tayoga.

"I don't need to pretend for the sake of practice that I am starving," he said. "I'm starving in fact and I do it without the need of applause."

"But Black Rifle was enjoying himself greatly," continued the Onondaga, "and we can rejoice in the joys of a friend. If we have not a thing ourselves it is pleasant to know that somebody else had it. He used his opportunities to the utmost. Here are more bones which he threw away, with shreds of flesh yet on them, and which the forest people came to pick clean. Lo, their tracks are everywhere about Black Rifle's little camp. One of them became so persistent and bold—a wolf it was—that Black Rifle, not willing to shoot, seized a large stone, and threw it at him with great violence. There lies the stone at the edge of the wood, and as there is fresh earth on its under surface it was partly imbedded in the ground where Black Rifle snatched it up. There, just beyond your right foot, Red Coat, is a little depression, the place in the earth, from which he tore it. Black Rifle's aim was good too. He struck the wolf. At the foot of the bank there are red stains where several drops of blood fell. The wolf was full of mortification, pain and anger, when he ran away. He would never have been so bold and venturesome, if his hunger had not made him forget his prudence. He was as hungry as you are this minute, Red Coat."

"I suppose you are giving me preliminary practice in torture, Tayoga. Well, go on with it, old fellow. I'll try to stand it."

"No, that is enough as a beginning. We will follow the trail of Black Rifle again. After he had eaten so well he was so much refreshed that he will start again with a vigorous and strong step. Lo, it is as I said! He is taking a long stride, but I do not think he is walking fast. His pace is very slow. It may be that there is something in what Dagaeoga says. It is possible that Black Rifle is waiting for those who will not be unwelcome to him."

Robert was quite able to fathom what was passing in the brain of the Onondaga. He saw that the trail was growing quite fresh, and his spirits became buoyant.

"And Red Coat is hungry," said Tayoga, that lurking gleam of humor in his eye growing larger. "Let him remember that however he may suffer from lack of food he can suffer yet more. It is wonderful what the body can endure and yet live. Here Black Rifle stopped and rested on these stones, perhaps an hour. No, Red Coat, there are no signs to show it, but the trail on the other side is much fresher, which proves it. It is quite clear now that Black Rifle is waiting. He is not running away from anybody or anything. Ah! Red Coat, if we only had some of his precious bear steaks how welcome to us they would be!"

"Go on, Tayoga. As I told you, I'd try to stand it."

"That is well, Red Coat. But it is not enough merely to wish for Black Rifle's bear steaks. We will have a portion of them ourselves."

"Now, Tayoga, your talk sounds a little wild to me."

"But listen, Red Coat."

The Onondaga suddenly put his fingers to his lips, and blew a shrill whistle that penetrated far in the forest. In a few instants, the answer, another whistle, came back from a point a few hundred yards ahead, and Tayoga said quietly:

"Red Coat, Black Rifle is waiting for us. We will now go forward and he will give us our dinner."

They advanced without hesitation and the figure of the dark hunter rose up to meet them. His face showed pleasure, as he extended his hand first to Willet.

"Dave, old comrade," he said, "the sight of you in the forest is always a pleasure to the eye. I thought you'd be coming with the lads, and I've been making ready for you. I knew that Tayoga, the greatest trailer the world has ever known, would be sure to strike my traces, and that he'd read them like print. And here's Robert too, a fine boy, if I do say it to his face, and Lieutenant Grosvenor. You mayn't know me, Lieutenant, though I recall you, and I can tell you you're mighty lucky to fall into the hands of these three."

"I think so too," said Grosvenor earnestly.

"Red Coat is happy to see you," said Tayoga, "but he will be happier to see your bear."

"The Lieutenant is hungry," said Black Rifle. "Then come; there is enough for all."

"What made you wait for us?" asked Robert.

"You know how I roam the woods, doing as I please and under nobody's command. I found that Tandakora was by the lake with warriors and that St. Luc was not far away. Tandakora's men seemed to be trailing somebody, and hiding in the bushes, I spied on them. I was near enough to hear two warriors talking and I learned that it was you they were following. Then, coming on ahead, I left a trail for you to see. And I've got plenty of bear steaks already cooked for you."

"God bless you, Mr. Black Rifle," said Grosvenor fervently.

"Amen!" said Robert.

Black Rifle showed them his lair among dense bushes, and, after they had satisfied their hunger, the bear, divided in equal portions among all, was stored away in their knapsacks, Grosvenor luckily having retained his own as the Indians had not deprived him of it. They now had food enough for several days, and one great source of anxiety was removed.

"What had you found, Black Rifle?" asked Willet.

"St. Luc has a big force. He's throwing a sort of veil before Montcalm, while the Marquis fortifies to meet the attack of the British and Americans that all know is coming. Perhaps the Lieutenant can tell us most about that force!"

"It's to be a great one," said Grosvenor.

"And we'll go through to Quebec!" said Robert, his eyes flashing, his imagination at once alive. "We'll put out forever the fire that's always burning in the north and give our border peace."

"Easy, lads, easy!" said Willet. "A thing's never done until it's done. I feel pretty sure we'll do it, but we'll reckon with present difficulties first. It seems to me it's our duty now to follow St. Luc, and see what he means to do with his force. It's hard on you, Lieutenant, because you'll have to stay with us. You can't go back to Albany just yet."

Grosvenor glanced around at the unbroken forest. "I'm resigned," he said. "After that wonderful escape I'm ready for anything. I see that this is my great chance to become a scout, and I'll do the best I can."

"I take it," said Black Rifle, "that the main object of St. Luc is to clear the forest of all our scouts and skirmishers in order that we may be kept in complete ignorance of Montcalm's movements. We'll show him that he can't do it. You have not forgotten any of your skill, have you, Tayoga?"

"So far from forgetting any of it he's acquired more," said Willet, answering for the Onondaga. "When it comes to trailing that boy just breathes it in. He adds some new tricks every day. But I think we'd better lie by, the rest of to-day, and to-night, don't you, Black Rifle? We don't want to wear out our lads at the start."

"Well spoken, Dave," responded Black Rifle. "It's a camp in the enemy's country we'll have to make with the warriors all about us, but we must take the risk. We'd better go to the next brook and walk up it a long distance. It's the oldest of all tricks to hide your trail, but it is still the best."

They found the brook only a few hundred yards farther on, and extended their walk along its pebbly bed fully a mile and a half as a precaution, keeping to their wading until they could emerge on rocky ground, where they left no trail.

"It will be only chance now that will bring them down on us," said Willet. "Do you think, Lieutenant, that after such a long walk you could manage another bear steak?"

"If the company will join me!" replied Grosvenor. "I don't wish to show bad manners."

"I'll join you," said Willet, speaking for the others, "and I think we'll make a brief camp on that wooded hill there."

"Why on a hill, Mr. Willet? Why not in a hollow where it seems to me we would be better hidden?"

"Because, besides hiding ourselves, we want to see, and you can see better from a height than from a valley. In the bushes there we'll have a view all about us, and I don't think our enemies can come too near, unseen by us. When we get into the thicket on the hill,

Lieutenant, you can resume that pleasant nap that you did not finish. Eight or ten hours more of sleep will be just the thing for you."

"All of you sleep a while," said Black Rifle. "I'll guard. I'm fresh. But be sure you walk on the stones. We must leave no trace."

They found a fairly comfortable place in the thicket and soon all were asleep except Black Rifle, who sat with his rifle between his knees, and from his covert scanned the forest on all sides.

Black Rifle felt satisfaction. He was pleased to be with the friends for whom he cared most. An historical figure, solitary, aloof, he was a vivid personality, yet scarcely anything was known about him. His right name even had disappeared, and, to the border, far and near he was just Black Rifle, or Black Jack, a great scout and a terror to the Indians. In his way, he was fond of Willet, Tayoga and young Lennox, and he felt also that he would like Grosvenor when he knew him better. So, while they slept, he watched with a vigilance that nobody save Tayoga could surpass.

Black Rifle saw the life of the forest go on undisturbed. The birds on the boughs went about their business, and the little animals worked or played as usual in the bushes. Everything said to him that no enemy was near, and his own five senses confirmed it. The afternoon passed, and, about twilight, Tayoga awoke, but the others slept on.

"Sleep now, Black Rifle," said the Onondaga. "I will take up the watch."

"I don't feel like closing my eyes just yet, Tayoga," replied the scout, "and I'll sit a while with you. Nothing has happened. Tandakora has not been able to find our trail."

"But he will hunt long for it, Black Rifle. When my race hates it hates well. Tandakora feels his grudge against us. He has tried to do us much harm and he is grieved because we have not fallen before him. He blames us for it."

"I know he does. Did you hear something walking in the thicket at the bottom of the hill?"

"It is only a bear. Perhaps he is looking for a good place in which to pass the night, but he will go much farther away."

"Why, Tayoga?"

"Because the wind is shifting about a little, and, in another minute, it will take him a whiff of the human odor. Then he will run away, and run fast. Now he is running."

"I don't hear him, Tayoga, but I take it that you know what you are saying is true."

"My ears are uncommonly keen, Black Rifle. It is no merit of mine that they are so. Why should a man talk about a gift from Manitou, when it really is the work of Manitou? Ah, the bear is going toward the south and he is well frightened because he never stops to look back, nor does he hesitate! Now he is gone and he will not come back again!"

Black Rifle glanced at the Onondaga in the dusk, and his eyes were full of admiration.

"You have wonderful gifts, Tayoga," he said. "I don't believe such eyes and ears as yours are to be found in the head of any other man."

"But, as I have just told you, Black Rifle, however good they may be the credit belongs to Manitou and not to me. I am but a poor instrument."

"Still you find 'em useful, and the exercise of such powers must yield a certain pleasure. They're particularly valuable just now, as I'm thinking we'll have an eventful night."

"I think so too, Black Rifle. With the warriors and the French so near us it is not likely that it could pass in peace."

"At any rate, Dave and the lads are not worrying about it. I never saw anybody sleep more soundly. I reckon they were pretty well worn out."

"So they were, and, unless danger comes very close, we will not awaken them. That it will be near us soon I do not doubt because Tododaho warns me that peril is at hand."

He was looking up at the star on which his patron saint sat and his face had that rapt expression which it always wore when his spirit leaped into the void to meet that of the great Onondaga chief who had gone away four hundred years ago. Black Rifle regarded him with respect. He too was steeped in Indian lore and belief, and, if Tayoga said he saw and heard what others could not hear or see, then he saw and heard them and that was all there was to it.

"What do you see, Tayoga?" he asked.

"Tododaho sits on his star with the wise snakes, coil on coil in his hair, and the great Mohawk, Hayowentha, who is inferior only to Tododaho, speaks to him from his own star across infinite space. They are talking of us, but it comes only as a whisper, like the dying voice of a distant wind, and I cannot understand their words. But both the great warriors look down warningly at us. They tell us to beware, that we are threatened by a great peril. I can read their faces. But a mist is passing in the heavens. The star of the Mohawk fades. Lo, it is gone! And now the vapors gather before the face of Tododaho too. Lo, he also has gone, and there are only clouds and mists in the far heavens! But the great chiefs, from their stars, have told us to watch and to watch well."

"I believe you! I believe every word you say, Tayoga," exclaimed Black Rifle, in a tone of awe. "The mist is coming down here too. I think it's floating in from the lake. It will be all over the thickets soon. I reckon that the danger threatening us is from the warriors, and if we are in a veil of fog we'll have to rely on our ears. I'm not bragging when I say that mine are pretty good, but yours are better."

Tayoga did not reply. He knew that the compliment was true, but, as before, he ascribed the credit to Manitou because he had made the gift and not to himself who was merely an involuntary agent. The mist and vapors were increasing, drifting toward them in clouds from the lake, a vanguard of shreds and patches, already floating over the bushes in which they lay. It was evident that soon they would not be able to see five yards from there.

In ten minutes the mist became a fog, white and thick. The sleeping three were almost hidden, although they were at the feet of the watchers, and the two saw each other but dimly. They seemed to be in a tiny island with a white ocean circling about them. The Onondaga lay flat and put his ear to the earth.

"What do you hear, Tayoga?" whispered the scout.

"Nothing yet, Black Rifle, but the usual whispers of the wilderness, a little wind among the trees and a distant and uneasy deer walking."

"Why should a deer be walking about at this time, and why should he be uneasy, Tayoga? Any deer in his right mind ought to be taking his rest now in the forest."

"That is true, Black Rifle, but this deer is worried and when a deer is worried there is a cause. A deer is not like a man, full of fancies and creating danger when danger there is none. He is troubled because there are strange presences in the woods, presences that he dreads."

"Maybe he scents us."

"No, the wind does not blow from us toward him. Do not move! Do not stir in the least, Black Rifle! I think I catch another sound, almost as light as that made by a leaf when it falls! Ah, Manitou is good to me! He makes me hear to-night better than I ever heard before, because it is his purpose, I know not why, to make me do so! There comes the little sound again and it is real! It was a footstep far away, and then another and another and now many! It is the tread of marching men and they are white men!"

"How do you know they are white men, Tayoga?"

"Mingled with the sound of their footsteps is a little clank made by the hilts of swords and the butts of pistols striking against the metal on their belts. There is a slight creaking of leather, too, which could not possibly come from a band of warriors. I hear the echo of a voice! I think it is a command, a short, sharp word or two such as white officers give. The sounds of the footsteps merge now, Black Rifle, because the men are marching to the same step. I think there must be at least fifty of them. They are sure to be French, because we are certain our troops are not yet in this region, and because only the French are so active that they make these swift marches at night."

"Unfortunately that's so, Tayoga. Will they pass near us?"

"Very near us, but I do not think they will see us, as the fog is so thick."

"Should we wake the others and move?"

"No, at least not yet. Now they are going very slowly. It is not because they do not know the way, but because the fog troubles them. It is St. Luc who leads them."

"I don't see how your ear can tell you that, Tayoga."

"It is not my ear, it is my mind that tells me, Black Rifle. The French would not go through the forest to-night, unless they had warriors with them as guides, flankers and skirmishers. Only St. Luc could make them come, because we know that even the French have great trouble in inducing them to enter big battles. They like better ambush and foray. De Courcelles could not make them march on this journey nor could Jumonville. My reason tells me it could be only St. Luc. It must be!"

"Yes, I'm sure now it's St. Luc up to some trick that we ought to meet."

"But we do not know what the trick is, Black Rifle. Ah, they have stopped! All of them have stopped!"

"It is not possible that they have seen any traces of us, Tayoga! We left no trail. Besides, this fog is so thick and heavy; it's like a blanket hiding everything!"

"No, it is not that. We left no trail. They are so near that we could see them if there were no fog. Now I hear some one walking alone in front of the company. His step is quick, sharp and positive. It is St. Luc, because, being the leader, he is the only one who would walk that way at such a time. I think he wants to see for himself or rather feel just where they are. Now he too stops, and some one walks forward to join him. It is a Frenchman, because he has on boots. I can hear just the faintest creak of the leather. It must be De Courcelles."

"It may be his comrade Jumonville."

"No, it is De Courcelles, because he is tall while Jumonville is not, and the stride of this man who is going forward to join St. Luc is long. It is surely De Courcelles. St. Luc does not like him, but he has to use him, because the Frenchmen are not many, and a leader can only lead those who are at hand to be led. Now they talk together. Perhaps they are puzzled about the direction."

"Well, so would I be if I had to go anywhere in such a fog."

"They walk back together to the soldiers, and now there is no noise of footsteps."

"I take it that they're waiting for something."

"Aye, Black Rifle. They are waiting in the hope that the fog will rise. You know how suddenly a fog can lift and leave everything bright and clear."

"And they would see us at once. They'll be fairly on top of us."

"So they would be, if the fog should go quickly away."

"And do you think it will?" asked Black Rifle in alarm.

Tayoga laughed under his breath.

"I do not," he replied confidently. "There is no wind to take it away. The great bank of mist and vapor will be heavy upon the ground and will increase in thickness. It would not be wise for us to move, because there may be ears among them as keen as ours, and they might hear us. Then blinded by the fog we might walk directly into the hands of prowling warriors. Although we are not many yards from them we are safest where we are, motionless and still."

Black Rifle also lay down and put his ear to the earth.

"I hear very well myself, although not as well as you, Tayoga," he whispered, "and I want to notice what they're doing as far as I can. I make out the sound of a lot of footsteps, but I can't tell what they mean."

"They are sending groups in different directions, Black Rifle, looking for a way through the forest rather than for us. They are still uncertain where they are. Five or six men are going southward, about as many have turned toward the west, and two warriors and a Frenchman are coming toward us, the rest stay where they are."

"It's the three coming in our direction who are bothering me."

"But remember, Black Rifle, that we are hidden in the deep fog as a fish is hidden in the water, and it will be almost as hard to find us. They must step nearly upon us before they could see us."

Black Rifle, in his eventful life upon the border, had passed through many a crisis, but never any that tested his nerves more thoroughly than the one he now faced. He too heard the steps of the three warriors coming in their direction, cautiously feeling a way through the great bank of mist. It was true that they could pass near without seeing, but chance might bring them straight to the little group. He shifted his fingers to the lock and trigger of his rifle, and looked at the sleeping three whose figures were almost hidden, although they were not a yard away. He felt that they should be awake and ready but in waking, Grosvenor, at least, might make enough noise to draw the warriors upon them at once.

"They have shifted their course a little," whispered Tayoga, "and it leads to our right. Now they change back again, and now they keep turning toward the left. I think they will pass eight or ten yards from us, which will be as good as five hundred or a thousand."

The white man slowly raised his rifle, but did not cock it. That action would have made a clicking sound, sharp and clear in the fog, but the quick hands were ready for instant use. He knew, as Tayoga had said, that the chance of the warriors walking upon them in the blinding fog was small, but if the chance came it would have to be met with all their power and resource.

"I think they will come within about ten feet of us," continued Tayoga, in his soft whisper. "There are two tall warriors and one quite short. The tall ones take about three steps to the short one's four and even then the short man is always behind. They do not walk in single file as usual, but spread out that they may cover as much ground as possible. Now they are coming very near and I think it best, Black Rifle, that I talk no more for the present, but I will hold my rifle ready as you are doing, if unlucky chance should bring them upon us."

The footsteps approached and passed a little to the left, but came so near that Black Rifle almost fancied he could see the dim figures in the fog. When they went on he drew a mighty breath and wiped the perspiration from his face.

"We fairly grazed the edge of death," he whispered. "I'll sit up now and you can do the rest of the listening all by yourself, Tayoga."

"The three have rejoined the main body," said the Onondaga, "and the other parties that went out have also gone back. I think the one that went south probably found the way in which they wanted to go, and they will now move on, leaving us safe for the while. Yes, I can hear them marching and the clank of the French weapons and equipment."

He listened a few minutes longer, and then announced that they were quite beyond hearing.

"They are gone," he said, "and Great Bear, Dagaeoga, and Red Coat have not even known that they were here."

"In which they were lucky," said Black Rifle.

The scout awoke the three, who were much astonished to learn that such danger had passed so near them. Then they considered what was best for them to do next.

CHAPTER VII.
THE FOREST BATTLE

"It is quite evident," said Robert, as they talked, "that we must follow on the trail of St. Luc. We've settled in our minds that he wants to keep our people busy along Lake George, while Montcalm fortifies higher up. Then it's our duty to find out what he's doing and stop it if we can."

All were in agreement upon the point, even Grosvenor, who did not yet feel at home in the woods.

"But we must wait until the fog lifts," said Willet. "If we moved now we might walk directly into the arms of the enemy, and we can afford to wait the night through, anyhow. Tayoga, we have got to keep you fresh, because your senses and faculties must be at their finest and most delicate pitch for trailing, so now you go to sleep. All the rest of you do the same, and I'll watch."

Soon four slumbered, and only the hunter was awake and on guard. But he was enough. His sight and hearing were almost as good as those of Tayoga himself and he too began to believe that the Onondaga's Manitou was a shield before them. Danger had come often and very near, but it had always passed, and, for the present, at least, he was not apprehensive. The fog might hang on all night if it chose. They could easily make up lost ground in the morning. Meanwhile they were accumulating fresh strength. The four were sleeping very placidly, and it was not likely that they would awake before dawn. Willet looked at their relaxed figures with genuine benevolence. There were the friends for whom he cared most, and he felt sure the young Englishman also would become an addition. Grosvenor was full of courage and he had already proved that he was adaptable. He would learn fast. The hunter had every reason to be satisfied with himself and the situation.

The fog did not go away. Instead, it thickened perceptibly, rolling up in new waves from the lake. The figures of the sleeping four were wrapped in it as in a white blanket, but Willet knew they were there. No air stirred, and, as he sat silent, he listened for sounds that might come through the white veil, hearing only the occasional stirring of some animal. Toward morning the inevitable change occurred. A wind arose in the south, gentle puffs in the beginning, then blowing steady and strong. The fog was torn away first at the top, where it was thinnest, floating off in shreds and patches, and then the whole wall of it yielded before the insistent breeze, driven toward the north like a mist, and leaving the woods and thickets free. Willet made a careful circle about the camp, at a range of several hundred yards, and found no sign of hostile presence. Then he resumed his silent vigil, and, an hour later, the sun rose in a shower of gold. Tayoga opened his eyes and Willet awakened the others.

"The fog is gone," said the hunter, "and eyes are useful once more. I've been around the camp and there is no immediate threat hanging over us. We can enjoy a good breakfast on Black Rifle's cold bear, and then we'll start on St. Luc's trail."

The path of the force that had marched past in the night was quite plain. Even Grosvenor, with his inexperience, could tell that many men had walked there. Most of the Frenchmen as well as the Indians had worn moccasins, but the imprints made by the boot heels of De Courcelles and Jumonville were clearly visible among the fainter traces.

"How many men would you say were in this force, Tayoga?" asked Willet.

"About fifty Frenchmen and maybe as many warriors," replied the Onondaga. "The Frenchmen stay together, but the warriors leave now and then in little parties, and the trail also shows where some of the parties came back. See, Red Coat, here is where two warriors returned. The French stay with St. Luc, not because they are not good scouts and trailers, but because the division of the work now allots this task to the Indians."

"You're right when you call the French good scouts and trailers," said Willet. "They seem to take naturally to forest life, and I know the Indians like them better than they do any other white people. As I often tell Robert, here, the French are enemies of whom anybody can be proud. There isn't a braver race in the world."

"I don't underrate 'em," said Grosvenor.

"It won't be long until we reach their camp," said Tayoga. "Sharp Sword is too great a leader to have carried his men very far in a blind fog. I do not think he went on more than a mile. It is likely that he stopped at the first brook, and the slope of the ground shows that we will come soon to a stream. More of the scouts that he sent out are returning to the main trail. They could not have gone far in the fog and of course they found nothing."

"We'll have, then, to beware lest we run into their camp before they've left it," said Willet.

"I don't think Sharp Sword would stay there after dawn," continued the Onondaga. "The fact that he marched at night in the fog shows that he is eager to get on, and I am quite sure we will find a cold camp. Here go the footsteps of St. Luc. I know they are his, because his foot is small and he wears moccasins. All the French soldiers have larger feet, and the other two Frenchmen, De Courcelles and De Jumonville, wear boots. Sharp Sword does not regard the two officers with favor. He does not associate with them more than is necessary. He keeps on the right side of the trail and they on the left. Here go his moccasins and there go their boots."

"And straight ahead is the brook by the side of which we'll find their camp," said Robert, who had caught the silver flash of water through the green foliage.

The trail, as he had said, led to the brook where the signs of an encampment were numerous.

"The fog was dense with them as it was with us," said Tayoga. "It is shown by the fact that they moved about a great deal, walking over all the ground, before they finally chose a place. If there had been no fog or even only a little they could have chosen at once what they wanted. Knowing that they had no enemy strong enough to be feared they kindled a fire here by this log, more for the sake of light than for warmth. Sharp Sword did not talk over anything with his lieutenants, De Courcelles and Jumonville. His trail leads to the north side of the camp, where he wrapped himself in his blanket and lay down. I imagine that the Canadian, Dubois, who goes with him, as an attendant, watched over him. De Courcelles and Jumonville slept on the other side of the camp. There go their boots. All the French soldiers but Dubois lay down to sleep, and only the warriors watched. They left at dawn, not stopping to eat breakfast. If they had eaten, birds would be here hunting shreds of flesh in the grass, but we do not see a single bird, nor has any wolf or other prowling animal been drawn by the odor of food. We were right in our surmise that Sharp Sword did not wish to delay. Perhaps there is some force of ours that he can catch in a trap, and he wishes to repeat his success against the Mountain Wolf."

"And it is our business to stop him," said Willet.

"If so, we must act promptly, Great Bear. When Sharp Sword makes up his mind to strike he strikes, quick and hard. After his brief camp here he continued his march toward the south. He threw out warriors as scouts and skirmishers. You can see their trail, leading off into the woods, and then his main force marched in a close and compact group. Just beyond the camp a little while after they made the new start he called De Courcelles and De Jumonville to him, and talked with them a little. Here is where his moccasins stood, and here is where their boots stood, facing him, while they received his orders. Then the boots walked back to the end of the line and St. Luc must have spoken to them very sharply."

"Why do you say that, Tayoga?" asked Grosvenor.

"You will notice that here where the trails of boots turn back the stems of grass in two or three places are broken off, not crushed down. De Courcelles and Jumonville kicked them in anger with the sharp toes of their boots, and they could have been angry only because Sharp Sword rebuked them."

"You must be right, Tayoga."

"It does not admit of any doubt, Red Coat. They took their places at the rear of the marching line, and Sharp Sword went on ahead. At no time does he permit them to walk beside him. He still regards the two Frenchmen with much disfavor, and he will continue to do so though he must use them in his expedition."

Tayoga spoke in his precise school English, in which he never omitted or abbreviated a word, but he was very positive. It did not occur to any of the others to doubt him. They had seen too many evidences of his surpassing skill on the trail. They swung along and Grosvenor noticed that many birds now appeared, hopping about in the path, as if searching among the bushes and in the grass for something.

"It looks as if they were seeking food dropped by our foes," he said.

"Did we not say that Red Coat would learn and learn fast!" exclaimed Tayoga. "He has in him the spirit of the forester, and, in time, he will make a great trailer. I have observed the birds, Red Coat, and your conclusion is correct. Sharp Sword's force did not pause to cook breakfast or even to eat it at the camp, but they took it as they walked along swiftly, dropping shreds of flesh or grains of hominy or bones picked clean as they walked. The birds have come to feast on their leavings. Doubtless, they have eaten all already and are merely hunting for more that does not exist. It is strange that no prowling wolf has come. Ah, I see the nose of one now in the thicket! Sharp Sword and his force cannot be very far ahead, and we shall have to be very cautious how we proceed."

"I think it likely," said Willet, "that Tandakora and his band will join him soon. If he is intending an attack upon us somewhere he will want to mass his full strength for it."

"Tandakora will join him before he makes his next camp," said Tayoga, in the most positive manner. "Great Bear reasons well. I expect to see the trail of the Ojibway chief, within an hour."

They went forward slowly, lest they walk into an ambush set by the foe, and, before they had gone two miles, the Onondaga pointed to a new trail coming out of the forest and merging into that of St. Luc.

"Dagaeoga knows who has walked here!" he said.

"Yes," replied Robert. "It's easy to tell where the great feet of Tandakora have passed. I suppose he leaves bigger footprints than any other man now in the province of New York. His warriors were with him too when he joined St. Luc. We were right in supposing that the French leader meditates an attack upon us somewhere."

"Tandakora talked a while with St. Luc," said Tayoga, when they had gone a hundred yards farther. "The big moccasins and the small moccasins stood together beside the trail. The earth was dampened much by the fog last night and it leaves the impressions. I think he talked longer with the Ojibway than he did with De Courcelles and Jumonville. Tandakora is an evil man but perhaps St. Luc feels less dislike for him than he does for the two white men. The Ojibway is only a savage from the region of the Great Lakes, but the Frenchmen should know that the straight way of life is the right way. You do not forget, Dagaeoga, how De Courcelles planned with the others that time we were in Quebec, to have you killed by the bully, Boucher!"

"I don't forget it," said Robert. "I can never forget it, nor do I forget how Dave took my place and sent the bully to a land where he can never more do murder. Much as I hate Tandakora, I don't blame St. Luc for hating him less than he does De Courcelles and Jumonville."

"After the talk they went on together to the head of the line," said Tayoga. "Now they increase their speed. The stride of St. Luc lengthens and as it lengthens so must those of all the rest. We are not now in any danger of running into them, but we may incur it before night."

They did not abate their own speed, but continued in the path without pause, until nearly noon. The broad trail led straight on, over hills, across valleys and always through deep forest, cut here and there by clear streams. The sun came out, and it was warm under the trees. Grosvenor, unused to such severe exertion of this kind, began to breathe with difficulty. But Tayoga called a halt in time at the edge of a brook, and all knelt to drink.

"St. Luc's men were tired and thirsty too, Red Coat," said the Onondaga. "All of them drank. You can see the prints of their knees and feet as they bent over the water. It is a good brook. Manitou has filled the wilderness with its like, that man and beast may enjoy them. We will rest here a while, if Great Bear and Black Rifle say so."

"We do," said the two men together.

They remained fully an hour by the little stream. Robert himself, used as he was to the wilderness, was glad of the rest, and Grosvenor fairly reveled in it, feeling that his nerves and muscles were being created anew. They also made further inroads on their bear and Grosvenor was glad to see the birds coming for the shreds they dropped. He had quite a kindly feeling for the little winged creatures.

"I don't want to think that everything in the woods is an enemy," he said.

When they resumed the pursuit they found another new trail merging into that of the main force. It was a mixed band, red and white as the character of the footprints showed, and numbered about twenty men.

"It is clear," said Tayoga, "that as we supposed, Sharp Sword is planning a heavy stroke. All the detached forces are coming in, under instructions, to join him. We know that Montcalm drew back into the north after his great blow at Fort William Henry, and we think he is going to fortify on Champlain or between the two lakes. Some of our people must be along the shores of Andiatarocte and Sharp Sword does not want them to find out too much about Montcalm."

"At any rate I think our own enterprise will culminate before night," said Willet. "We should overtake them by dusk if we try."

"Sharp Sword's men will make a new camp before long," said Tayoga, "and from that they will launch their attack upon whatever point or force of ours they intend to attack. They are not going so fast now, and the trail is growing very warm. Sharp Sword's stride is shortening and so, of course, is the stride of all the others. I think he now feels that the need of hurrying is over, and he is likely to become much more deliberate."

"And the ground is beginning to slope down toward a deep valley," said Willet. "Water and wood will be plentiful there, and I think that's where St. Luc will make his camp to-night."

"I think so too," said Tayoga. "And since the dusk is not far away maybe they have lighted the fire already. Suppose, Great Bear, we climb the hill on our right and see if our eyes can reach their smoke."

The crest of the hill was about three hundred feet above them, but when they reached it they could see a great distance on all sides, the lake a vast glittering bowl on their left and the mighty green wilderness of hills, mountains and woods on their right. Directly ahead of them was a faint dark line against the dazzling blue of the sky.

"Smoke!" said Tayoga.

"St. Luc's smoke," said Willet.

"The very smoke of the camp for which we were looking and which we were expecting!" said Black Rifle.

Robert's pulses beat hard, as they always did when he knew the great French Chevalier to be near. But that emotion soon passed and in its place came the thought of the enemy's presence. However much he admired St. Luc he was an official foe, to be met upon the battlefield.

"We must look into their camp," he said.

"So we must," said Willet, "and to do that we shall have to go much nearer. The risk is too great now, but it will soon be night, and then we can approach. We can see them well, then, because they'll build all the fires they like, since they think they have nothing to fear."

Then the five waited in silence among the thick woods on the crest of the hill, and Grosvenor prepared his mind for his first stalk. Full of courage, ambitious, eager to excel, he resolved to acquit himself with credit. But this was war, far different from that on the open fields of Europe for which his early training had fitted him. One must lie in the deep forest and depend upon the delicacy of eye and ear and an exceeding quickness of hand. It had not been long since he would have considered his present situation incredible, and, even now, it required some effort to convince himself that it was true.

But there beside him were the comrades whom he liked so well, Robert, Tayoga and the hunter whom he had known before and the strange dark figure of Black Rifle, that man of mystery and terror. Around him was the wilderness now in the glow of advancing twilight, and before him he knew well lay St. Luc and the formidable French and Indian force. Time and place were enough to try the soul of an inexperienced youth and yet Grosvenor was not afraid. His own spirit and willingness to dare peril made a shield for him. His comrades were only four in number, but Grosvenor felt that, in fact, they were twenty. He did not know what strange pass into which they would lead him, but he felt sure they would succeed.

He saw the red rim of the sun sink behind the western crests, and then the last twilight died into the night. Heavy darkness trailed over the forest, but soon moon and stars sprang out, and the sky became silver, the spire of smoke reappearing across its southern face. But Willet, who was in reality the leader of the little party, gave no sign. Grosvenor knew that they were waiting for the majority of St. Luc's force to go to sleep, leaving only the sentinels before they approached, but it was hard to sit there so long. His nerves were on edge and his muscles ached, but his spirit put a powerful rein over the flesh and he said never a word, until far in the night Willet gave the order to advance.

"Be careful, lads," he said, "and now is your chance, Lieutenant, to show how well you can keep up the start you've made as a trailer. That smoke over there which merges from several camp fires is our beacon."

They crept through the thickets. Grosvenor saw the dark gray tower against the sky grow larger and larger, and at last a luminous glow that came from the camp fires, rose under the horizon.

"To the edge of this last hill," whispered Willet, "and I think we can see them."

They redoubled their care as they advanced, and then, thrusting their heads through the bushes, looked down into the little valley in which the camp of St. Luc was pitched.

Several fires were burning, and Robert distinctly saw the French leader standing before one of them, not in forest green, but in his splendid officer's uniform of white and silver. A gallant and romantic figure he looked, outlined by the blaze, young, lithe and strong. Again the heart of the lad throbbed, and he was drawn powerfully toward St. Luc. What was it that caused this feeling and why had the Chevalier on more than one occasion and at risk shown himself to be his friend?

Not as many in the camp as they had expected had yet gone to sleep. Tandakora, somber and gigantic, gnawed the flesh from the big bone of a deer and then, throwing the bone into the fire, approached St. Luc. Robert saw them talking and presently De Courcelles and Jumonville came also. The four talked a little while and now and then the Chevalier pointed toward the south.

"That is where they intend their blow to fall," whispered Tayoga.

"Beyond a doubt, lad," the hunter whispered back, "but we may be able to anticipate 'em."

The wild scene, the like of which he had never looked upon before, cast a strange spell over Grosvenor. He too recognized, even at the distance, the power of St. Luc's personality, and Tandakora, looming, immense, in the firelight, was like some monster out of an earlier, primordial world. Warriors and soldiers asleep were scattered before the fires, and, at the edge of the forest, walked the sentinels. It was an alert and formidable camp, and the young Englishman felt that he and his comrades were grazing the extreme edge of danger.

De Courcelles and Jumonville presently left St. Luc and went to another fire, where they lay down and fell asleep, their military cloaks spread over them. Then the short, dark Canadian Dubois appeared and St. Luc spoke to him also. Dubois bowed respectfully and brought a blanket, which he spread before the fire. St. Luc lay down on it, and he too was soon asleep.

"It's time for us to go," whispered Willet, "but I'd feel safer if Tandakora also went to sleep. That savage is likely to send out scouts."

"Tandakora does not mean to sleep to-night," said Tayoga. "He suspects that we are somewhere near and he is troubled. If he were not uneasy he would take his rest, which is what a chief always does when the opportunity presents itself. But he has thrown his second bone into the fire, and he walks about, looking now at the sleepers and now at the forest. I think he will soon send two or three runners toward the south. See, he is speaking to them now, and two are starting."

Two Indians left the camp and glided silently into the woods. Then Tandakora stopped his restless pacing, and lay down on the ground. His face was in the shadow, but he seemed to be asleep.

The four on the hill crept away as cautiously as they had come, and they agreed that they would make a curve around St. Luc's camp, traveling all night toward the south. Willet was anxious about the two warriors whom Tandakora had sent out, and he felt that they might possibly encounter them on the way. He led his little group first toward the lake and then bore south, being quite sure that before noon the next day they would reach a British or American detachment of some kind. Everything indicated such proximity and they were agreed that they would find their friends on the shores of the lake. It was not likely that either colonials or regulars would leave the open water and go far into woods which furnished so many perils.

They were refreshed by sleep and plenty of food and they made good time. They walked in single file, Willet leading with Tayoga last and Grosvenor in front of him. The young Englishman's ambition, encouraged by success, was rising higher than ever, and he was resolved that this night trail which he was treading should be a good one, so far as he was concerned. Robert walked in front of him and he was careful to step exactly where young Lennox did, knowing that if he did so he would break no sticks and make no undue noise. The test was severe, but he succeeded. By and by his breath grew short once more. Nevertheless he was glad when Willet halted, and asked Tayoga if he heard any unusual sound in the forest. Before replying the Onondaga lay down and put his ear to the ground.

"I do hear a sound which is not that of the trees nor of an animal," he replied. "It is made by men walking, and I think they are the two warriors whom Tandakora sent out from the camp."

"And if you can hear them walking they must be very near. That is sure."

"It is true, Great Bear. These two warriors are sent south to spy upon whatever force of ours St. Luc means to attack, and it may be that they will strike our trail, although they are not looking for it. There is light enough now to show our traces to good trailers."

"Aye, Tayoga, you speak truly. Lie down, lads, we must not show ourselves. It's possible that they'll pass on and not dream of our presence here."

"It is in the hands of Manitou," said the Onondaga gravely. "They are still walking toward the south at an even pace, which shows that they have seen nothing. I can hear their footfalls, only a whisper against the earth, but unmistakable. Now, they are just behind us, and their course is the same as ours. Ah, the footfalls cease! They have stopped. They have seen our trail, Great Bear. Manitou has given his decree against us, and who are we to complain? He has done so much for us that now he would put us to the test, and see whether we are worthy of his favor. We shall have to fight the messengers."

"It should be easy enough for us who are five to beat two warriors," said Robert.

"We can surely beat two," said Tayoga, "but they will try to hold us while they call help. It will not be long before you hear the cry of a night bird, doubtless an owl."

"Have they begun to move again?" asked Robert.

"I cannot hear a sound. Perhaps they are stirring, but they creep so cautiously that they make no noise at all. It would be their object to make their own position uncertain and then we would go on at great peril from their bullets. It will be best for us to stay a while where we are."

Tayoga's words were accepted at once as wise by the others. It was impossible to tell where the two warriors now lay, and, if they undertook to go on, their figures would be disclosed at once by the brilliant moonshine. So they flattened themselves against the ground in the shadow of the bushes and waited patiently. The time seemed to Grosvenor to be forever, but he thrilled with the belief in coming combat. He still felt that he was in the best of all company for forest and midnight battle, and he did not fear the issue.

Willet was hopeful that the skies would darken, but they did not do so. The persistent moon and a host of stars continued to shine down, flooding the forest with light, and he knew that if any one of them stood up a bullet would be his instant welcome. At last came the cry of the night bird, the note of the owl, as Tayoga had predicted, rising from a point to their right and somewhat behind them, but too far away for rifle shot. It was a singular note, wild, desolate and full of menace.

"There may have been another band of warriors in this direction," whispered Tayoga, "perhaps a group of hunters who had not yet returned to St. Luc, and he is calling to them."

"No earthly doubt of it," said Black Rifle. "Can you hear the reply, Tayoga?"

"Now I hear it, though it is very faint. It is from the south and the warriors will soon be here. We shall have a band to fight."

"Then we'd better bear off toward the west," said Willet. "Come, lads, we have to creep for it."

They made their way very slowly on hands and knees away from the lake, Willet leading and Tayoga bringing up the rear. It was hard and painful work for Grosvenor, but again he succeeded in advancing without noise, and he began to think they would elude the vigilance of the savage scouts, when a sibilant whisper from Willet warned them to fall flat again. His command was just in time as a rifle cracked in the bushes ahead of them, and Grosvenor distinctly heard the bullet as it hissed over their heads. Willet threw his rifle to his shoulder but quickly took it down again. The Indian who had fired was gone and a little puff of smoke rising above the bushes told where he had been. Then the five crept away toward the right and drew into a slight hollow, rimmed around with bushes, where they lay hugging the earth.

"Our course took us almost directly into the path of that fellow," said Willet, "and of course he saw us. I'm sorry I didn't get a shot at him."

"Do not worry, Great Bear," said Tayoga. "You will find plenty of use for your bullets. The band has come. Hark to the war whoop!"

The long, piercing yell, so full of menace and most sinister in its dying note, swelled through the forest. Grosvenor, despite his courage and confidence in his comrades, shivered. He had heard that same yell many a time, when Braddock's army was cut down in the deep forest by an invisible foe. He could never forget its import. But he grasped his rifle firmly, and strove to see the enemy, who, he knew, was approaching. His four comrades lay in silence, but the muzzle of every weapon was thrust forward.

"It's fortunate we found this little hollow," said Willet. "It will give us shelter for a while."

"And we'll need it," said Black Rifle. "They know where we are, of course, but they'll take their time about attacking."

"Keep your heads down, lads," said Willet. "Don't be too eager to see. If they're too far away for us to shoot at we are too far away for them too."

Five minutes later and a flash came from a thicket on their left. Willet pulled trigger at the flash and a death cry came back.

"That's one out of the way," said Black Rifle calmly, "and they're mad clean through. Hear 'em yell!"

The fierce war whoop died in many echoes, and bullets spattered the rocks about them. The five made no further reply as yet, but the forest battle was now on.

CHAPTER VIII.
THE BOAT BUILDERS

Robert and Grosvenor lay, side by side, propped up partly on their elbows, their rifles thrust well forward, and watching toward the north. They were not able to see anything, save the dark outline of the forest, and a little puff of smoke rising where an Indian had fired. The wilderness itself was absolutely still but Robert's vivid imagination as usual peopled it thickly. Although his eye did not reach any human figure his mind pictured them everywhere, waiting patiently for a chance at his comrades and himself. He, more than any other of the five, realized the full extent of the danger. His extraordinary fancy pictured to him every possibility, and so his courage was all the greater, because he had the strength to face them with a tranquil mind.

A flash in the thicket and a bullet struck on a rock near Robert, glanced off and buried itself in a tree beyond them. He shivered a little. Fancy pictured the bullet not as missing, but as hitting him. Then he steadied himself, and was as ready as Willet or Black Rifle for whatever might come.

"I think that shot was fired by a sharpshooter who has crept forward ahead of the others," whispered the hunter. "He's lying behind that low bush to the west."

"I'm of your mind about it," said Black Rifle. "As soon as he reloads he'll chance another shot at where he thinks we're lying, and that will be his last."

Robert heard the low words, and he shivered again a little. He could never grow used to the taking of human life, even in dire necessity. He knew that Willet had spoken the truth, and that the red sharpshooter would fire only one more shot. Soon he had the proof. The second flash came from the same point. Again the bullet glanced among the rocks, but, before the report of the rifle died, another answered. It was that of the hunter and he found his mark. A cry came from the bush, followed by a fierce yell of anger from those farther back, and then the sinister stillness settled again over the wilderness.

"The Indian has gone!" whispered Grosvenor in an awed tone to Robert.

"Yes, Dave fired at the flash, and he never misses. The cry showed it. But it will make the warriors all the more eager to take us."

The silence lasted about a quarter of an hour, and then fire was opened upon them from three sides, bullets singing over their heads, or spattering upon the rocks.

"Lie flat, lads," commanded Willet. "This is random lead, and if we keep close to the earth 'twill all pass us by. The warriors are seldom good marksmen."

But one of the bullets, glancing from a rock, nipped Black Rifle in the shoulder. It was a very slight wound, though, and its only effect was to make him more eager to reach his enemy. In a few minutes his chance came as he caught a glimpse of a dusky but incautious figure among the trees, and, quick as a flash, drew trigger on it. There was no cry, but he saw the shadowy figure go down, not to rise again, and the fierce soul of Black Rifle was satisfied.

Scattered shots were fired, after another silence, and a bullet grazed the back of Grosvenor's hand, drawing a drop or two of blood. It stung for a few moments, but, on the whole, he was proud of the little hurt. It was a badge of honor, and made him truly a member of this great forest band. It also stimulated his zeal, and he became eager for a shot of his own. He watched intently and when the warriors fired again he sent his bullet at the flash, as he had seen Willet and Black Rifle do. He did not know whether he had hit anything, but he hoped. Tayoga, who fired for the first time presently brought down a warrior, and Robert wounded another. But Willet and Black Rifle talked together in whispers and they were anxious.

"They won't try to rush us so long as we keep among the rocks," said the hunter. "They know now that we're good shots, but they'll hold us here until day when their main force will come up and then we'll be finished."

"It seems pretty certain that's their plan now," said the scout, "and between you and me, Dave, we've got to get away from here somehow. The moon has faded a bit, and that will help us a little. What do you think, Tayoga?"

"We did not escape other traps to remain here in this," replied the Onondaga. "We must take the chance and go."

"In half an hour, perhaps. When the clouds floating up there get well before the moon."

Robert heard them distinctly and he glanced at the moon which was steadily growing paler, while the shadows were deepening over the forest. Yet it was obvious that it would not become very dark, and the ha'f hour of which Willet had spoken would probably measure the limit of the increase.

"Can you hear them moving in the bush, Tayoga?" asked Willet.

The Onondaga put his ear to the ground.

"Only a light sound toward the north reaches me," he replied. "Warriors there seem to be moving about. It may be that they have received more help. I think, Great Bear, that the time for us to go, if we go at all, is coming fast."

Willet decided in a few minutes that it would not be any darker than it was then; and, choosing a southern direction, he crept from the rocks, the others following him in line, Tayoga as usual bringing up the rear. They made a hundred yards in silence, and, then, at a low signal from the hunter, they sank down, almost flat, every one listening for a sound from the besiegers. Only Tayoga was able to hear faint noises to right and left.

"They do not know yet that we have left the rocks," he whispered, "and they are still watching that point. Manitou may carry us in safety between them."

They were about to resume their painful creeping, when a half dozen rifles on their right flashed, and they dropped down again. But the bullets did not come their way, instead they rang among the rocks which they had just left. Tayoga laughed softly.

"They think we are still there," he whispered, "and they send much lead against the inoffensive stone. The more the better for us."

"I'm devoutly glad the rocks catch what is intended for us," said Grosvenor, feeling intense relief. "How long do you think it will be, Tayoga, before I can stand up and walk like a man again?"

"No one can answer that question," replied the Onondaga. "But remember, Red Coat, that you are getting splendid practice in the art of going silently along a trail on a dark night. It is what every forest runner must learn."

Grosvenor in the dusk could not see the twinkle in Tayoga's eye, but, drawing upon fresh founts of courage and resolution, he settled himself anew to his task. His elbows and knees ached and it was difficult to carry his rifle as he crawled along, but his ambition was as high as ever, and he would not complain. The lone hoot of an owl came from the point on the right, where one of the Indian groups lay, and it was promptly answered by a like sound from the left where another group was hidden.

"I think they're beginning to suspect that we may have slipped away," said Willet, "and they're talking to one another about it. Now they'll stalk the rocks to see, but that will take time, which we can use handily. Come on, lads, we'll go as fast as possible."

Curving around a small hill, Willet rose to his feet and the others, with intense relief, did likewise. Robert's and Grosvenor's joints were young and elastic, and the stiffness quickly left them, but both had done enough creeping and crawling for one night. All stood listening for a minute or two. They heard no more shots fired at the rocks, but the two owls began to call again to each other.

"Do you understand them, Tayoga?" asked Willet.

"They talk the Huron language," replied the Onondaga, in his precise fashion, "that is, their signals are those used by the Hurons. They are asking each other what has happened at the rocks, and neither can tell. Their expression is that of doubt, impatience and worry. They say to each other: 'Those whom we believed we held in a trap may have broken out of it. It will take time to see and also much peril if they are still in the trap, because they can use their rifles well.' We annoy them much, Great Bear."

The big hunter chuckled.

"I don't mind that," he said. "Their worries are not my worries. Ah, there they go again! What are they saying now, Tayoga?"

"Their tone grows more anxious. You can tell what they feel by the expression of the owl. Their fear that we may have stolen out of the trap is increasing, but they cannot know unless they go and see, and then they may be creeping into the muzzles of our rifles. It is a difficult problem that we have given them to solve, Great Bear."

"We'll leave it for 'em, lads. Now that we're on our feet we'll go at speed."

They walked very rapidly, but they stopped when they heard once more the faint cries of the owls, now almost lost in the distance. Tayoga interpreted them.

"They are cries of anger," he said. "They have discovered that we are not in the rocks, and now they will look around for our trail, which will be hard to find in the darkness of the night."

"And the thing for us to do is to keep on toward the south as hard as we can."

"So it would be, Great Bear, but others are coming up from the south, and we would go directly into their arms."

"What do you mean, Tayoga?"

"A number of men are advancing, and I think they are warriors."

"Then we have merely slipped out of one trap to fall into another."

"It is possible, Great Bear. It is also possible that those who come are friends. Let me put my ear to the earth, which is the bringer of sound. It is clear to me that those who walk toward us are warriors. White men would not tread so lightly. I do not think, Great Bear, that any force of the Indians who are allied with the French would be coming up from the south, and the chances are that these be friends."

He sent forth the call of a bird, a beautiful, clear note, and it was answered instantly with a note as clear and as beautiful.

"They are friends!" said Tayoga joyfully. "These be the Ganeagaono!"

"Ganeagaono?" exclaimed Grosvenor.

"Mohawks," explained Robert. "The Keepers of the Eastern Gate. The leading warriors of the Six Nations and friends of ours. We are, in truth, in luck."

Ten dusky figures came forward to meet them, and with great joy Robert recognized in the leader the fierce young Mohawk chief, Daganoweda, who once before had come to their help in a crisis. But it was Tayoga who welcomed him first.

"Daganoweda, of the clan of the Turtle, of the nation, Ganeagaono, of the great League of the Hodenosaunee, the sight of you is very pleasant to our eyes," he said.

"Tayoga, of the clan of the Bear, of the Nation, Onondaga, of the great League of the Hodenosaunee, you are my brother and we are well met," the chief rejoined.

They saluted each other and then Daganoweda greeted the others, all of whom were known to him of old save Grosvenor, but who was presented duly in the ceremonious style loved by the Iroquois.

"We are pursued by men of Tandakora," said Willet. "They are not far away now. We do not wish to fight them because we would hasten below with a warning."

The black eyes of the fierce Mohawk flashed.

"Will the Great Bear give us his battle?" he said.

He asked for it as if for a favor.

"We usually fight our own quarrels through," replied Willet, "but as I said, duty calls us from here in haste. Then, since you wish it, Daganoweda, we pass the fight to you. But have you enough men?"

"Ten Mohawks are enough to meet any wandering band of our enemies that may be in the woods," replied the young chief, proudly. "Let Great Bear and his friends go in peace. This fight is ours."

Despite the dusk, Robert saw Daganoweda's eyes glisten. He thoroughly understood the fierce soul of the young Mohawk chief, who would not let such a brilliant opportunity for battle pass him.

"Then farewell, Daganoweda," said Willet. "You have been a friend at the right moment."

He led again in the flight toward the south and the five saw the chief and his warriors passing the other way sink into the dusk. Soon they heard shots behind them and they knew that the Mohawks were engaged in battle with the Hurons and their friends. They sped on for a long time, and when they stopped they were close to the shores of the lake, the water showing dimly through the trees.

"I think we may rest easy for a while now," said Willet. "I'm certain not one of those warriors was able to get by the Mohawks, and it's not likely that an enemy is within several miles of us. Can you hear anything, Tayoga?"

"Nothing," replied the Onondaga. "Tododaho, on his star, tells me that we have this part of the forest to ourselves."

"That being so, we'll stay here a long time. Lads, you might unroll your blankets and make the best of things."

Grosvenor's blanket had not been taken from him when he was a prisoner, and it was still strapped on his back. He and Robert found the rest most welcome and they were not slow in wrapping the blankets around their bodies and making themselves comfortable. Without willing it, they fell asleep, but were awakened shortly after dawn.

"See!" said Willet, pointing toward the south.

A filmy trail of blue smoke rose across the clear, blue sky.

"That, whatever it is," said the hunter, "is what St. Luc is advancing against, but in spite of all the risks we've run we'll be there in time to give warning."

Robert looked with the deepest interest at the smoke, which was a long way off, but it seemed to rise from the lake's edge and he thought it must be a British or American post. It was at a most exposed and dangerous point, but his heart thrilled at Willet's words. Yes, in spite of every danger that had been thrown across their path, they would be able to carry word in time.

"We'll be there in half an hour, and we'll know what's going forward," said Willet.

"We'll know before then," said Grosvenor confidently. "Our marvelous Indian friend here will tell us when we're half way."

Tayoga smiled, but said nothing, and they started again, Willet, as usual, leading, and the Onondaga bringing up the rear. The spire of smoke thickened and darkened, and, to Robert and Grosvenor, it seemed most friendly and alluring. It appeared to rise from a little point of land thrust into the lake but they could not yet see its base, owing to an intervening hill. Just before they reached the crest of the hill Tayoga said:

"Wait a moment, Great Bear. I think I hear a sound from the place where the smoke rises, and we may be able to tell what it means."

They stopped promptly, and the Onondaga put his ear to the earth.

"I hear the sounds very distinctly now," he said. "They are of a kind not often occurring on these shores."

"What are they?" asked Robert eagerly.

"They are made by axes biting into wood. Many men are cutting down trees."

"They're building a fort, and they're in a hurry about it or they would not be felling trees so early in the morning."

"Your reasoning about the hurry is good, Dagaeoga. The white man will not go into the forest with his ax at daybreak, unless the need of haste is great, but it is not a fort they build. Mingled with the fall of the axes I hear another note. It is a humming and a buzzing. It is heard in these forests much less often than the thud of the ax. Ah! I was in doubt at first, but I know it now! It is the sound made by a great saw as it eats into the wood."

"A saw mill, Tayoga!"

"Yes, Dagaeoga, that is what it is, and now mind will tell us why it is here. The logs that the axes cut down are sawed in the mill. The saw would not be needed if the logs were to be used for building a fort. The ax would do it all. The logs are being turned into planks and boards."

"Which shows that they're being used for some purpose requiring much finer finish than the mere building of a fort."

"Now the mind of Dagaeoga is working well. Great Bear and I have been on the point where the new saw mill stands."

"And the timber there is fine," interrupted Willet.

"Just the kind that white men use when they build long boats for traveling on the lakes, boats that will carry many men and armband supplies. We know that a great army of red coats is advancing. It expects to come up George and then probably to Champlain to meet Montcalm and to invade Canada. It is an army that will need hundreds of boats for such a purpose, and they must be built."

"And they're building some of 'em right here on this point, before us!" exclaimed Robert.

Tayoga smiled.

"It is so," he said precisely. "There cannot be any doubt of it. A saw mill could not be here for any other purpose. But if we had not come it would be destroyed or captured before night by St. Luc."

"Come on, lads, and we'll soon be among 'em," said Willet.

From the crest of a hill they looked down upon a scene of great activity. The sun was scarcely risen but more than fifty men were at work on the forest with axes, and, at the very edge of the water, a saw mill was in active operation. Along the shore, where as many more toiled, were boats finished and others in all stages of progress. Soldiers in uniform, rifles on shoulder, walked about.

It was a pleasant sight, refreshing to the eyes of Robert and Grosvenor. Here were many men of their own race, and here were many activities, telling of great energy in the war. After so much peril in the forest they would be glad to be in the open and with their own kind again.

"Look, Robert," said Willet, "don't you know them?"

"Know whom?" asked young Lennox.

"The officers of this camp. The lads in the brave uniforms. If my eyes make no mistake, and they don't make any, the fine, tall young fellow standing at the edge of the water is our Philadelphia friend, Captain Colden."

"Beyond a doubt it is, Dave, and right glad am I to see him, and there too is Wilton, the fighting Quaker, and Carson also. Why this is to be, in truth, a reunion!"

Willet put his hands to his mouth trumpet fashion, and uttered a long, piercing shout. Then the five advanced and marched into the camp of their friends, where they received a welcome, amazed but full of warmth, Grosvenor, too, being made to feel at home.

"Have you dropped from the skies?" asked Colden.

"Scarcely that," replied Robert, laughing with pleasure, "but we've been shot out of the forest, and very glad we are to be here. We've come to tell you also that we've been pursued by a strong French and Indian force, led by St. Luc himself, and that it will be upon you before nightfall."

"And I, trained in my boyhood not to fight, will have to fight again," said Wilton.

"I know that none will do it better," said Robert.

"But we will give you breakfast," said Colden, "and while you are eating I will put the camp in a posture of defense. We are here building boats to be used by the army in its advance against Montcalm, and we didn't know that the enemy in force was south of Crown Point."

There were several sheds and in one of these a most abundant breakfast was served to them, including coffee and white bread, neither of which they had seen in a long time, and which were most welcome. While they ate, they saw the young Pennsylvania officers arranging their forces with skill and rapidity.

"They've learned a lot since we were with 'em that time at Fort Refuge," said Robert.

"They've had to learn," said Willet. "The forests in these times are a hard teacher, but they're bright and good boys, just the same. Nobody would learn faster."

"Even as Red Coat has learned to be a scout and to know the trail," said Tayoga, "but he is not sorry to come among white men and to have good food once more."

"No, I'm not," said Grosvenor emphatically. "My ambition to be a fine trailer was high last night, and it's still with me, but I had enough of creeping and crawling to last me a long time, and if we have to fight again I think I can fight better standing up."

"We will have to fight again. Be sure of that," said Tayoga decisively.

Before breakfast was over Colden came to them, and Robert told, in detail and with great vividness, all they had seen. The young Philadelphia captain's face became very grave.

"It was you who warned us before Fort Refuge," he said, "and now you come again. You helped us to success then, and you'll help us now. Even if your coming does bring news of danger I'll consider it a good omen."

"We'll be proud to stand in line with you once more," said Robert, although he felt that, with St. Luc in command, the attack of the French and Indians would be formidable. Colden would have available for battle between one hundred and fifty and two hundred men, about fifty of whom were soldiers. But all the others, the boat builders and the rest, were capable fighters too. They could certainly make a powerful resistance even to the daring and skillful French Chevalier, and, with a certain number of boats finished, the lake also was open to them, in case retreat became necessary. Luckily, too, St. Luc had no cannon. Courageous Captain Colden considered their situation far from desperate. There was hope too that Daganoweda and his Mohawks might come, not only those he had with him in the night battle, but others as well. The Mohawks, loving a combat, would not let go by such a one as that now threatening.

Willet rose from his breakfast and surveyed the position. There were no real buildings, only sheds, the largest covering the saw mill, and the others used for the protection of tools and of the men, when they slept, against the weather. All the trees for a distance well beyond rifle shot had been cut away for timber, a lucky fact, as the hostile Indians could not now use them for ambush. Stout arms were throwing the fallen trees into a long line of breastworks, and the place already began to look like a fortified point. Willet's eyes glistened.

"Although St. Luc beat us when we were with Rogers," he said, "I think we'll hold him here. We've certain advantages that will help us mightily."

"Thanks to you and your comrades for bringing us such timely warning," repeated Colden. "I'll confess that I did not suspect any enemy was nearer than Champlain, and neither we nor our superiors at Albany have feared an attack here."

"It's sure to come," said Willet.

Grosvenor, refreshed and reinvigorated, was taking an active share in the preparations. He had smoothed and brushed his uniform with scrupulous care, and despite the great hardships through which he had passed, looked once more neat and trim. He had returned to his incarnation as a trim young British officer. Adaptable and liking the Americans, equipped moreover with a certain experience of the border, he was at once on the best of terms with Colden, Wilton, Carson and the others, and was, in truth, one of them. Wilton found him a belt and a small sword, which he buckled on, and which as a badge of office gave him a certain moral strength, making him in fact a thoroughly happy man that morning.

Black Rifle, after food, had slid quietly into the forest to spy out the enemy. Robert, flexible, vivid, his imagination always alive, was with Tayoga, helping him with the breastworks, and keeping an eye at the same time on the forest. The lake behind him stretched away, vast, peaceful and beautiful, but he seldom looked at it now. He did not anticipate danger that way. It would come through the woods.

A gradual slope, hemmed in on either side by high cliffs and only a few hundred yards wide, led to the point on which the saw mill stood. St. Luc must approach by the slope. The cliffs were impossible, and, the longer he looked at it, the better Robert liked the position. Daring men such as Colden had could hold it against a much larger force. Let St. Luc come, he would find a brave and ready defense.

"Dagaeoga thinks we can hold the saw mill even against Sharp Sword," said Tayoga.

"How do you know I think it?"

"Because it is printed on Dagaeoga's face. When Dagaeoga's fancy is alive, which is nearly all the time, his eyes speak and they tell one very clearly what he thinks. His eyes say that the slope is narrow; St. Luc can come that way only; we have here more than one hundred and fifty good rifles; and in face of the storm of lead that we can send against him he cannot rush us. That is what the eyes and face of Dagaeoga say."

"You're right, Tayoga, that is what my brain thinks, though I didn't know it was printed on my face. But it's all the easier for you to read it, because you're probably thinking the same that I do."

"I do, Dagaeoga. Since St. Luc is not able to effect a surprise, he has a great task before him, though he will persist in it, because he wants to destroy our force and our boats also."

But the morning passed without any demonstration from the forest. Many of the boat builders began to believe it was a false alarm, and murmured at the continuous and hard labor on the breastworks, but Colden, knowing that Willet and his friends were to be trusted implicitly, held them to their tasks. The hunter also looked into the question of food supply and found it ample. They had brought much food with them from Albany and the forest had furnished much more. There was no occasion for alarm on that point, since the siege could not be a long one. Noon came and no sign of the enemy. Willet began to think the attack would be postponed until night, as St. Luc doubtless had learned already that he could not carry the place by surprise. But he relied most upon the word of Black Rifle who had not yet returned from the forest. The dark scout came back about the middle of the afternoon, and he told Colden and Willet that he had seen nothing of Daganoweda and his Mohawks, though there were indications in the forest that they had defeated the Hurons the night before. But St. Luc Was at hand, not much more than a mile away, where he had pitched a camp. More French and Canadians had arrived and he now led a force of at least five hundred men, the great majority of whom were warriors. He thought an attack would be made after dark, but in what form it was impossible to say.

"Which means," said Colden, "that I must have sentinels who will never relax their vigilance."

"Particularly as the night is going to be dark," said Willet. "There's a haze over the lake now, and the sun will set in a mist."

The twilight was heavy as he had predicted, and it was soon black on the mountains and the lake. But within the camp fires were burning, throwing a cheerful light, and many guards were posted. Crude but effective fortifications stretched all along the forest side of the camp, and Willet, Black Rifle and Tayoga were among the stumps in front of them. No enemy would be able to hide there even in the night. Wagons in which they had brought their supplies were drawn up in a circle, and would form an inner line of defense. Robert was with Grosvenor and Wilton near the center of the camp.

"Knowing the French and Indians as I now do," said Wilton, "I never doubt for an instant that an attack will come before morning. My experience at Fort Refuge is sufficient indication. It is strange that I, who was reared not to believe in fighting, should now be compelled to do it all the time."

"And while my profession is fighting," said Grosvenor, "I always expected to fight in the open fields of Europe and now I'm learning my trade in the deep forests of North America, where it's quite another sort of business. How long do you think it will be, Lennox, before we hear the owls hoot and the wolves bark?"

Robert laughed.

"We've had a lot of such signals in the last few days," he replied, "but in this country battles are not always opened with 'em. Still, I dare say we'll hear 'em."

Out of the forest in front of them came a long, lonely hoot.

"Speak of the owl and you hear his voice," said Wilton.

"If Tayoga were here he could tell us exactly what that owl, who is no owl but an Indian, meant," said Grosvenor, "also the tribe of the Indian, his age, his complexion, what he had for supper, how he is feeling and whether he is married or single. Oh, I assure you, Wilton, you needn't smile! I've seen the Onondaga do things much more marvelous. Nothing short of trailing a bird through the air would really test his wilderness powers."

"I wasn't smiling at your belief, Grosvenor," said the young Quaker, "I was merely smiling at your earnestness. When you tell me anything about Tayoga's skill on the trail I shall believe it, I don't care what it is. I saw him do marvelous things when we were at Fort Refuge."

The owl ceased its melancholy cry, and no other sound came from the forest, while the camp waited, with as much patience as it could muster, for the attack.

CHAPTER IX.
THE MASKED ATTACK

Light clouds floated before the moon, and the surface of the lake was ruffled by a southern wind. As no attack was anticipated from the south, the guard in that quarter was comparatively small, but it was composed, nevertheless, of good men, the boat builders mostly, but all experienced with the rifle and under the direct command of Carson. But the main force was always kept facing the forest, and, there, behind the logs, Colden stood with the four—Black Rifle again being outside. The hooting of the owls had not been repeated and the long wait had become hard upon the nerves of the young Philadelphia captain.

"Do you feel sure that they will attack to-night?" he asked Willet. "Perhaps St. Luc, seeing the strength of our position, will draw off or send to Montcalm for cannon, which doubtless would take a week."

The hunter shook his head.

"St. Luc will not go away," he said, "nor will he send for cannon, which would take too long. He will not use his strength alone, he will depend also upon wile and stratagem, against which we must guard every minute. I think I'll take my own men and go outside. We can be of more service there."

"I suppose you're right, but don't walk into danger. I depend a lot on you."

Willet climbed over the logs. Tayoga, Robert and Grosvenor followed.

"Red Coat buckled on a sword, and I did not think he would go on a trail again," said Tayoga.

"One instance in which you didn't read my mind right," rejoined the Englishman. "I know that swords don't belong on the trail, but this is only a little blade, and you fellows can't leave me behind."

"I did read your mind right," said Tayoga, laughing softly. "I merely spoke of your sword to see what you would say. I knew all the time that you would come with us."

The stumps, where the forest had been cut away, stretched for a distance of several hundred yards up the slope, and, a little distance from the breastwork, the dark shadow of Black Rifle came forward to meet them.

"Nothing yet?" asked the hunter.

"Nothing so far. Three or four good men are with me among the stumps, but not a warrior has yet appeared. I suppose they know we'll be on watch here, and it's not worth while taking so great a risk."

They advanced to the far edge of the stump region and crouched there. The night was now quite dark, the moon almost hidden, the stars but few, and the forest a solid black line before them.

"Why can't Tayoga use his ears?" said Grosvenor. "He'll hear them, though a mile away."

"A little farther on and he will," replied Willet, "but we, in our turn, don't dare to go deep into the forest."

A hundred yards more and the Onondaga put ear to earth, but it was a long time before he announced anything.

"I hear footsteps fairly near to us," he said at last, "and I think they are those of warriors. They would be more cautious, but they do not believe we are outside the line of logs. Yes, they are warriors, all warriors, there is no jingle of metal such as the French have on their coats or belts, and they are going to take a look at our position. They are about to pass now to our right. I also hear steps, but farther away, on our left, and I think they are those of Frenchmen."

"Likely De Courcelles and Jumonville wanting also to look us over," said Willet.

"There is another and larger force coming directly toward us," continued the Onondaga, "and I think it includes both French and warriors. This may be the attack and perhaps it would be better for us to fall back."

They withdrew a little, but remained among the stumps, though hidden carefully. Robert himself could now hear the advance of the large force in front of them, and he wondered what could be St. Luc's plan of battle. Surely he would not try to take the sawmill by storm in face of so many deadly rifles!

Black Rifle suddenly left the others and crept toward the right. Robert's eyes followed him, and his mind was held by a curious sort of fascination. He knew that the scout had heard something and he almost divined what was about to occur. Black Rifle stopped a moment or two at a stump, and then curved swiftly about it. A dusky figure sprang up, but the war cry was choked in the throat of the Huron, and then the knife, wielded by a powerful arm, flashed. Robert quickly turned his eyes away, because he did not wish to see the fall of the blade, and he knew that the end was certain. Black Rifle came back in a few moments. His dark eyes glittered, but he had wiped the knife, and it was in his belt again.

"His comrades will find him in a few minutes," said Willet, "and we'd better not linger here."

"They went back toward the sawmill and presently they heard a terrible cry of rage, a cry given for the fallen warrior.

"I don't think I shall ever grow used to such yells," said Grosvenor, shuddering.

"I've never grown used to 'em yet," said Robert.

The shout was followed by a half dozen shots, and a bullet or two whistled overhead, but it was clear that all of them had been fired at random. The warriors, aware that the chance of surprise had passed, were venting their wrath in noise. Willet suddenly raised his own rifle and pulled the trigger. Another dusky figure sprang up and then fell prone.

"They were coming too close," he said. "That'll be a warning. Now back, lads, to the breastwork!"

As they retreated the shots and yells increased, the forest ringing with the whoops, while bullets pattered on the stumps. Both Grosvenor and Robert were glad when they were inside the logs once more, and Colden was glad to see them.

"For all I knew you had fallen," he said, "and I can't spare you."

"We left our mark on 'em," said the saturnine Black Rifle. "They know we're waiting for 'em."

The demonstration increased in volume, the whole forest ringing with the fierce whoops. Stout nerves even had good excuse for being shaken, and Colden paled a little, but his soul was high.

"Sound and fury but no attack," he said.

Willet looked at him approvingly.

"You've become a true forest leader, Captain Colden," he said. "You've learned to tell the real rush from the pretended one. They won't try anything yet a while, but they're madder than hornets, and they're sure to move on us later. You just watch."

Yet Colden, Wilton and the others were compelled to argue with the men, especially with the boat builders and wood choppers. Stern military discipline was unknown then in the forest; the private often considered himself a better man than his officer, and frequently told him so. Troops from the towns or the older settled regions seemed never to grow used to Indian methods of warfare. They walked again and again into the same sort of ambush. Now, they felt sure, because the Indian fire had evaporated in scattered shots, that the French and the warriors had gone away, and that they might as well be asleep, save for the guards. But Colden repressed them with a stern hand.

"If it hadn't been for our experience at Fort Refuge I might feel that way myself," he said. "The silence is certainly consoling, and makes one feel that all danger has passed."

"The silence is what I dread most," said Robert. "Is anything stirring on the lake?"

"Not a thing," replied Wilton, who had been watching in that quarter. "I never saw George look more peaceful."

Robert suggested that they go down to the shore again, and Wilton, Grosvenor and he walked through the camp, not stopping until they stood at the water's edge.

"You surely don't anticipate anything here," said Wilton.

"I don't know," replied Robert, thoughtfully, "but our enemies, both French and Indians, are full of craft. We must guard against wile and stratagem."

Wilton looked out over the lake, where the gentle wind still blew and the rippling waters made a slight sighing sound almost like a lullaby. The opposite cliffs rose steep and lofty, showing dimly through the dusk, but there was no threat in their dark wall. To south and north the surface melted in the darkness, but it too seemed friendly and protecting. Wilton shook his head. No peril could come by that road, but he held his peace. He had his opinion, but he would not utter it aloud against those who had so much more experience than he.

The darkness made a further gain. The pallid moon went wholly out, and the last of the stars left. But they had ample wood inside the camp and they built the fires higher, the flames lighting up the tanned eager faces of the men and gleaming along the polished barrels of their long rifles. Willet had inspected the supply of ammunition and he considered it ample. That fear was removed from his mind.

Tayoga went to the edge of the forest again, and reported no apparent movement in the force of St. Luc. But they had built a great fire of their own, and did not mean to go away. The attack would come some time or other, but when or how no man could tell.

Robert, who could do as he pleased, concluded to stay with Wilton on the shore of the lake, where the darkness was continually creeping closer to the shore. The high cliffs on the far side were lost to sight and only a little of Andiatarocte's surface could now be seen. The wind began to moan. Wilton shivered.

"The lake don't look as friendly as it did an hour ago," he said.

A crash of shots from the slope followed his words. The war whoop rose and fell and rose again. Bullets rattled among the stumps and on the crude stockade.

"The real attack!" said Wilton.

"Perhaps," said Robert.

He was about to turn away and join in the defense, but an impulse from some unknown source made him stay. Wilton's duty kept him there, though he chafed to be on the active side of the camp. The sharp crack of rifles showed that the defenders were replying and they sent forth a defiant cheer.

"They may creep down to the edge of the stumps and try to pick off our men," said Robert, "but they won't make a rush. St. Luc would never allow it. I don't understand this demonstration. It must be a cover for something else."

He looked thoughtfully into the darkness, and listened to the moan of the lake. Had the foe a fleet he might have expected an attack that way, but he knew that for the present the British and Americans controlled Andiatarocte.

The darkness was still gathering on the water. He could not see twenty yards from the land, but behind him everything was brightness. The fires had been replenished, the men lined the stockade and were firing fast. Cheers replied to whoops. Smoke of battle overhung the camp, and drifted off into the forest. Robert looked toward the stockade. Again it was his impulse to go, and again he stayed. There was a slight gurgling in the water almost at his feet, and a dark figure rose from the waves, followed in an instant by another, and then by many more. Robert, his imagination up and leaping, thrilled with horror. He understood at once. They were attacked by swimming savages. While the great shouting and turmoil in their front was going on a line of warriors had reached the lake somewhere in the darkness, and were now in the camp itself.

He was palsied only for a moment. Then his faculties were alive and he saw the imminent need. Leaping back, he uttered a piercing shout, and, drawing his pistol, he fired point blank at the first of the warriors. Wilton, who had felt the same horror at sight of the dark faces, fired also, and there was a rush of feet as men came to their help.

The warriors were armed only with tomahawk and knife, and they had expected a surprise which they might have effected if it had not been for Robert's keenness, but more of them came continually and they made a formidable attack. Sending forth yell after yell as a signal to their comrades in front that they had landed, they rushed forward.

Neither Robert nor Wilton ever had any clear idea of that fierce combat in the dark. The defenders fired their rifles and pistols, if they had time, and then closed in with cold steel. Meanwhile the attack on the front redoubled. But here at the water's edge it was fiercest. Borderer met warrior, and now and then, locked in the arms of one another, they fell and rolled together into the lake. Grosvenor came too, and, after firing his pistols, he drew his small sword, plunging into the thick of the combat, thrusting with deadly effect.

The savages were hurled back, but more swimming warriors came to their aid. Dark heads were continually rising from the lake, and stalwart figures, almost naked, sprang to the shore. Tomahawks and knives gleamed, and the air echoed with fierce whoop of Indian and shout of borderer. And on the other side of the camp, too, the attack was now pressed with unrelenting vigor. The shrill call of a whistle showed that St. Luc himself was near, and Frenchmen, Canadians and Indians, at the edge of the cleared ground and in the first line of stumps, poured a storm of bullets against the breastwork and into the camp.

Many of the defenders were hit, some mortally. The gallant Colden had his fine three cornered hat, of which he was very proud, shot away, but, bare-headed, calm and resolute, he strode about among his men, handling his forces like the veteran that he had become, strengthening the weak points, applauding the daring and encouraging the faltering. Willet, who was crouched behind the logs, firing his rifle with deadly effect, glanced at him more than once with approval.

"Do you think we can hold 'em off, Tayoga?" the hunter said to the Onondaga, who was by his side.

"Aye, Great Bear, we can," replied Tayoga. "They will not be able to enter our camp here, but this is not their spearhead. They expect to thrust through on the side of the water, where they have come swimming. Hark to the shouts behind us!"

"And the two lads, Robert and the young Englishman, have gone there. I think you judge aright about that being their spearhead. We'll go there too!"

Choosing a moment when they were not observed by the others, lest it might be construed as a withdrawal in the face of force, they slipped away from the logs. It was easy to find such an opportunity as the camp was now full of smoke from the firing, drifting over everything and often hiding the faces of the combatants from their comrades only a few yards away.

But the battle raged most fiercely along the water's edge. There it was hand to hand, and for a while it looked as if the dusky warriors would make good their footing. To the defenders it seemed that the lake spewed them forth continually, and that they would overwhelm with weight of numbers. Yet the gallant borderers would not give back, and encouraging one another with resounding cheers they held the doubtful shore. Into this confused and terrible struggle Willet and Tayoga hurled themselves, and their arrival was most opportune.

"Push 'em back, lads! Push 'em back! Into the water with 'em!" shouted the stalwart hunter, and emptying rifle and pistol he clubbed the former, striking terrific blows. Tayoga, tomahawk in hand, went up and down like a deadly flame. Soldiers and borderers came to the danger point, and the savages were borne back. Not one of them coming from the water was able to enter the camp. The terrible line of lead and steel that faced them was impassable, and all the time the tremendous shouts of Willet poured fresh courage and zeal into the young troops and the borderers.

"At 'em, lads! At 'em!" he cried. "Push 'em back! Throw 'em into the water! Show 'em they can't enter our camp, that the back door, like the front door, is closed! That's the way! Good for you, Grosvenor! A sword is a deadly weapon when one knows how to use it! A wonderful blow for you, Tayoga! But you always deal wonderful ones! Careful, Robert! 'Ware the tomahawk! Now, lads, drive 'em! Drive 'em hard!"

The men united in one mighty rush that the warriors could not withstand. They were hurled back from the land, and, after their fashion when a blow had failed, they quit in sudden and utter fashion. Springing into the water, and swimming with all their power, they disappeared in the heavy darkness which now hovered close to shore. Many of the young soldiers, carried away by the heat of combat, were about to leap into the lake and follow them, but Willet, running up and down, restrained their eager spirits.

"No! No!" he cried. "Don't do that. They'll be more'n a match for you in the water. We've won, and we'll keep what we've won!"

All the warriors who had landed, save the dead, were now gone, evidently swimming for some point near by, and the battle in front, as if by a preconcerted signal, also sank down suddenly. Then St. Luc's silver whistle was heard, and French and Indians alike drew off.

Robert stood dazed by the abrupt end of the combat. His blood was hot, and millions of black specks danced before his eyes. The sudden silence, after so much shouting and firing, made his pulses beat like the sound of drums in his ears. He held an empty pistol in his right hand, but he passed his left palm over his hot face, and wiped away the mingled reek of perspiration and burned gunpowder. Grosvenor stood near him, staring at the red edge of his own sword.

"Put up your weapon, Red Coat," said Tayoga, calmly. "The battle is over—for the time."

"And we've won!" exclaimed Grosvenor. "I could hardly believe it was real when I saw all those dark figures coming out of the water!"

Then he shuddered violently, and in sudden excess of emotion flung his sword from him. But he went a moment later and picked it up again.

The attack had been repulsed on every side, but the price paid was large. Fifteen men were dead and many others were wounded. The bodies of seventeen Indians who had fallen in the water attack were found and were consigned to the waves. Others, with their French allies, had gone down on the side of the forest, but most of the fallen had been taken away by their comrades.

It was a victory for Colden and his men, but it left serious alarm for the future. St. Luc was still in the forest, and he might attack again in yet greater force. Besides, they would have to guard against many a cunning and dangerous device from that master of forest warfare. Colden called a council, at which Willet and Black Rifle were central figures, and they agreed that there was nothing to be done but to strengthen their log outworks and to practice eternal vigilance. Then they began to toil anew on the breastworks, strengthening them with fresh timber, of which, fortunately, they had a vast supply, as so much had been cut to be turned into boats. A double guard was placed at the water's edge, lest the warriors come back for a new attack, and the wounded were made as comfortable as the circumstances would admit. Luckily Willet and many others were well acquainted with the rude but effective border surgery, much of it learned from the Indians, and were able to give timely help.

The hurt endured in silence. Their frontier stoicism did not allow them to give voice to pain. Blankets were spread for them under the sheds or in the sawmill, and some, despite their injuries, fell asleep from exhaustion. Soldiers and borderers walked behind the palisades, others continually molded bullets, while some were deep in slumber, waiting their turn to be called for the watch.

It began to rain by and by, not heavily, but a slow, dull, seeping fall that was inexpressibly dreary, and the thick, clammy darkness, shot with mists and vapors from the lake, rolled up to the very edge of the fires. Robert might have joined the sleepers, as he was detached from immediate duty, but his brain was still too much heated to admit it. Despite his experience and his knowledge that it could not be so, his vivid fancy filled forest and water with enemies coming forward to a new attack. He saw St. Luc, sword in hand, leading them, and, shaking his body violently, he laughed at himself. This would never do.

"What does Dagaeoga see that is so amusing?" asked Tayoga.

"Nothing, Tayoga. I was merely ridiculing myself for looking into the blackness and seeing foes who are not there."

"And yet we all do it. If our enemies are not there they are at least not far away. I have been outside with Black Rifle, and we have been into the edge of the forest. Sharp Sword makes a big camp, and shows all the signs of intending to stay long. We may yet lose the sawmill. It is best to understand the full danger. What does Dagaeoga mean to do now?"

"I think I'll go back to the water's edge, and help keep the watch there. That seems to be my place."

He found Wilton still in command of the lake guard, and Grosvenor with him. The young Quaker had been shocked by the grim battle, but he showed a brave front nevertheless. He had put on his military cloak to protect himself from the rain, and Robert and Grosvenor had borrowed others for the same purpose.

"We've won a victory," said Wilton, "but, as I gather, it's not final. That St. Luc, whose name seems to inspire so much terror, will come again. Am I not right, Lennox?"

"You're right, Wilton. St. Luc will come not a second time only, but a third, and a fourth, if necessary."

"And can't we expect any help? We're supposed to have command of this lake for the present."

"I know of none."

The three walked up and down, listening to the mournful lapping of the waves on the beach, and the sigh of the dripping rain. The stimulus of excited action had passed and they felt heavy and depressed. They could see only a few yards over the lake, and must depend there upon ear to warn them of a new attack that way. The fact added to their worries, but luckily Tayoga, with his amazing powers of hearing, joined them, establishing at once what was in effect a listening post, although it was not called then by that name. Wilton drew much strength from the presence of the Onondaga, while it made the confidence of Grosvenor supreme.

"Now we'll surely know if they come," he said.

A long while passed without a sign, but they did not relax their vigilance a particle, and Tayoga interpreted the darkness for them.

"There was a little wind," he said, after a while, "but it is almost dead now. The waves are running no longer. I hear a slight sound to the south which was not there before."

"I hear nothing, Tayoga," said Robert.

"Perhaps not, Dagaeoga, but I hear it, which is enough. The sound is quite faint, but it is regular like the beating of a pulse. Now I can tell what it is. It is the stroke of a paddle. There is a canoe upon the lake, passing in front of us. It is not the canoe of a friend, or it would come at once to the land. It contains only one man. How do I know, Red Coat? Because the canoe is so small. The stroke of the paddle is light and yet the canoe moves swiftly. A canoe heavy enough to hold two men could not be moved so fast without a stroke also heavy. How do I know it is going fast, Dagaeoga? Do not ask such simple questions. Because the sound of the paddle stroke moving rapidly toward the north shows it. Doubtless some of Sharp Sword's warriors brought with them a canoe overland, and they are now using it to spy upon us."

"What can we do about it, Tayoga?"

"Nothing, Red Coat. Ah, the canoe has turned and is now going back toward the south, but more slowly. The man in it could locate our camp easily by the glow of the fires through the mist and vapors. Perhaps he can see a dim outline of our figures."

"And one of us may get a bullet while we stand here watching."

"No, Red Coat, it is not at all likely. His aim would be extremely uncertain in the darkness. The warrior is not usually a good marksman, nor is it his purpose here to shoot. He would rather spy upon us, without giving an alarm. Ah, the man has now stopped his southward journey, and is veering about uncertainly! He dips in the paddle only now and then. That is strange. All his actions express doubt, uncertainty and even alarm."

"What do you think has happened, Tayoga?"

"Manitou yet has the secret in his keeping, Dagaeoga, but if we wait in patience a little it may be revealed to me. The canoe is barely moving and the man in it watches. Now his paddle makes a little splash as he turns slightly to the right. It is certain that he has been alarmed. The spy thinks he is being spied upon, and doubtless he is right. He grows more and more uneasy. He moves again, he moves twice in an aimless fashion. Although we do not see him in the flesh, it is easy to tell that he is trying to pierce the darkness with his eyes, not to make out us, but to discern something very near the canoe. His alarm grows and probably with good cause. Ah, he has made a sudden powerful stroke, with the paddle, shooting the canoe many feet to the left, but it is too late!"

"Too late for what, Tayoga?" exclaimed Robert.

The Onondaga did not reply for a moment or two, but stood tense and strained. His eyes, his whole attitude showed excitement, a rare thing with him.

"It was too late," he repeated. "Whatever threatened the man in the canoe, whatever the danger was, it has struck. I heard a little splash. It was made by the man falling into the water. He has gone. Now, what has become of the canoe? Perhaps the warrior when he fell dropped the paddle into the water, and the canoe is drifting slowly away. No, I think some one is swimming to it. Ah, he is in the canoe now, and he has recovered the paddle! I hear the strokes, which are different from those made by the man who was in it before. They have a longer sweep. The new man is stronger. He is very powerful, and he does not take the canoe back and forth. He is coming toward the land. Stand here, and we will welcome Daganoweda of the Ganeagaono. It might be some other, but I do not think it possible. It is surely Daganoweda."

A canoe shot from the mists and vapors. The fierce young Mohawk chief put down the paddle, and, stepping from the light craft into the shallow water, raised his hand in a proud salute. He was truly a striking figure. The dusk enlarged him until he appeared gigantic. He was naked except for belt and breech cloth, and water ran from his shining bronze body. A tomahawk and knife in the belt were his only weapons, but Robert knew instinctively that one of them had been wielded well.

"Welcome, Daganoweda," he said. "We were not looking for you, but if we had taken thought about it we might have known that you would come."

The dark eyes of the Mohawk flashed and his figure seemed to grow in stature.

"There has been a battle," he said, "and Sharp Sword with a great force is pressing hard upon the white brothers of the Ganeagaono. It was not possible for Daganoweda to stay away."

"That is true. You are a great chief. You scent the conflict afar, and you always come to it. Our people could have no truer, no braver ally. The arrival of Daganoweda alone is as the coming of ten men."

The nostrils of the chief dilated. Obviously he was pleased at Robert's round and swelling sentences.

"I come in the canoe of a foe," he said. "The warrior who was in it has gone into the lake."

"We know that. Tayoga, who is a wonder for hearing, and a still greater wonder at interpreting what he hears, followed your marvelous achievement and told us every step in its progress. He even knew that it was you, and announced your coming through the mists and vapors."

"Tayoga of the clan of the Bear, of the nation Onondaga, of the great League of the Hodenosaunee, is a great warrior, and the greatest trailer in the world, even though he be so young."

Tayoga said nothing, and his face did not move, but his eyes gleamed.

"Do you come alone?" asked Robert.

"The warriors who were with me when you met us in the woods are at hand," replied the chief, "and they await my signal. They have crept past the line of Sharp Sword, though Tandakora and many men watched, and are not far away. I will call them."

He sent forth twice the harsh cry of a water fowl. There was no answer, but he did not seem to expect any, standing at attention, every line of his figure expressing supreme confidence. The others shared his belief.

"I hear them. They come," said Tayoga at length.

Presently a slight sound as of long, easy strokes reached them all, and in a few moments a line of dark heads appeared through the mists and vapors. Then the Mohawks swam to land, carrying their rifles and ammunition, Daganoweda's too, on their heads, and stood up in a silent and dripping line before their chief.

"It is well," said Daganoweda, looking them over with an approving eye. "You are all here, and we fight in the next battle beside our white brothers."

"A battle that you would be loath to miss and right glad we are to welcome such sturdy help," said the voice of Willet behind them. "I'll tell Captain Colden that you're here."

The young captain came at once, and welcomed Daganoweda in proper dignified fashion. Blankets and food were given to the Mohawks, and they ate and warmed themselves by the fire. They were not many, but Robert knew they were a great addition. The fiery spirit of Daganoweda alone was worth twenty men.

"I think that we'd better seek sleep now," said young Lennox to Grosvenor. "I admit one is tempted to stay awake that he may see and hear everything, but sooner or later you've got to rest."

They found a good place under one of the sheds, and, wrapped in blankets, soon sank to slumber. The day after such a momentous night came dark and gloomy, with the rain still dripping. A north wind had arisen, and high waves chased one another over the lake. There was still much fog on the land side, and, under its cover, the French and Indians were stalking the camp, firing at every incautious head.

"Most of those bullets are French," said Tayoga, "because the warriors are not good sharpshooters, and they are aimed well. I think that Sharp Sword has selected all the best French and Canadian marksmen and has sent them down to the edge of the woods to harass us. As long as the fog hangs there we may expect their bullets."

The fire of these hidden sharpshooters soon became terribly harassing. From points of vantage they sent their bullets even into the very heart of the camp. Not a head or a shoulder, not an arm could be exposed. Three men were killed, a dozen more were wounded, and the spirit of the garrison was visibly affected. At the suggestion of Willet, Colden selected thirty sharpshooters of his own and sent them among the stumps to meet the French and Canadian riflemen.

Robert and Tayoga were in this band, and Willet himself led it. Daganoweda and three of his warriors who were good shots also went along. Black Rifle was already outside on one of his usual solitary but fierce man-hunts. All the men as soon as they left the breastworks lay almost flat on the wet ground, and crept forward with the utmost care. It was a service of extreme danger, none could be more so, and it was certain that not all of them would come back.

CHAPTER X.
IN THE FOG

When Robert went into the fog and began to creep from stump to stump, his imagination leaped up at once and put a foe at every point in front of him. Perhaps he deserved more credit for courage and daring than any of the others, because his vivid fancy foresaw all the dangers and more. Tayoga was on his right and Willet on his left. Daganoweda, who had all the eagerness of Black Rifle himself, was farther down the line. Flashes of fire appeared now and then in the fog ahead of them, and bullets hummed over their heads.

Robert, essentially humane, began to share, nevertheless, the zeal of these hunters of men around him. The French and Canadians were seeking their lives and they must strike back. He peered through the fog, looking for a chance to fire, forgetting the wet ground, and the rain which was fast soaking him through and through. He was concerned only to keep his rifle and powder dry. Two flashes on his right showed that the defenders were already replying.

"We cannot go much farther, Dagaeoga," whispered Tayoga, "or we will be among them. I shall take this stump just ahead."

"And I the one beside it. I don't mind admitting that a thick stump between you and your enemy is a good thing."

He sank down behind his chosen bulwark, and stared through the fog. The flashes of fire continued, but they were on his right and left, and nothing appeared directly in front of him. A cry came from a point farther down the line. One of the defenders had been hit and presently another fell. Robert again saw all the dangers and more, but his mind was in complete command of his body and he watched with unfailing vigilance. He saw Willet suddenly level his rifle across his protecting stump and fire. No cry came in response, but he believed that the hunter's bullet had found its target. Tayoga also pulled trigger, but Robert did not yet see anything at which to aim, although the sound of shots from the two hostile fronts was now almost continuous.

The combat in the dim mists had a certain weird quality and Robert's imaginative mind heightened its effect. It was almost like the blind shooting at the blind. A pink dot would appear in the fog, expand a little, and then go out. There would be a sharp report, the whistling of a bullet, perhaps, and that was all. The white men fought in silence, and, if there were any Indians with the French and Canadians they imitated them.

Robert, at last, caught a glimpse of a dusky figure about thirty yards in front of him, and, aiming his rifle, quickly fired. He had no way of knowing that he had hit, save that no shot came in reply, but Tayoga, who was once again ear to the ground, said that their foes were drawing back a little.

"They find our fire hotter than they had expected," he said. "If they can shoot in the fog so can we, and the Great Bear is more than a match for them in such a contest."

The whole line crept forward and paused again behind another row of stumps. A general volley met them and they found protection none too soon. Bullets chipped little pieces off the stumps or struck in the ground about them. But Robert knew that they had been fired largely at random, or had been drawn perhaps by a slight noise. There was a strong temptation to return the fire in a like manner, but he had the strength of mind to withhold his aim for the present, and not shoot until he had a sure target.

Yet the dim battle in the fog increased in volume. More skirmishers from the forces of St. Luc came up, and the line of fire spread to both left and right. A yell was heard now and then, and it was evident that the Indians in large numbers were coming into the combat. Willet's band was reënforced also from the camp, and his line extended to meet that of the foe. Rifles cracked incessantly, the white fog was sprinkled with pink dots, and, above the heads of the men, it was darkened by the smoke that rose from the firing. At rare intervals a deep cheer from a borderer replied to the savage war whoop.

A man four stumps from Robert was hit in the head and died without a sound, but Willet, firing at the flash of the rifle that slew him, avenged his loss. A bullet grazed Robert's head, cutting off two locks of hair very neatly. Its passage took his breath for a moment or two, and gave him a shock, but he recovered quickly, and, still controlling his impulse to pull trigger in haste, looked for something at which to aim.

The fog had not lifted at all, but by gazing into its heart a long time, Robert was able to see a little distance. Now and then the figure of an enemy, as he leaped from the shelter of one stump to another, was outlined dimly, but invariably there was not enough time for a shot. Soon he made out a large stump not very far ahead of him, and he saw the flash of a rifle from it. He caught a glimpse only of the hands that held the weapon, but he believed them to be a white man's hands and he believed also that the man behind the stump was one of the best French sharpshooters.

Robert resolved to bring down the Frenchman, who presently, when firing once more, might then expose enough of himself for a target. He waited patiently and the second shot came. He saw the hands again, the arms, part of one shoulder and the side of the head, and taking quick aim he pulled the trigger, though he was satisfied that his bullet had missed.

But the flame of battle was lighted in Robert's soul. Hating nobody and wishing good to all, he nevertheless sought to kill, because some one was seeking to kill him, and because killing was the business of those about him. What came to be known later as mass psychology took hold of him. All his mental and physical powers were concentrated on the single task of slaying an enemy. The affair now resolved itself into a duel between single foes.

Deciding to await a third shot from his enemy, he made his position behind the stump a little easier, poised, as it were, ready to throw every faculty, physical and mental, into his reply to that expected third shot. He was quite sure, too, that he would have a chance, because the man had exposed so much more of himself at the second shot than at the first, and his escape from the bullets would make him expose yet more at the third. His heart began to throb hard, and his pulses were beating fast. The battle was still going on about him, but he forgot all the rest of it, the shots, the shouts, the flashes, and remembered only his own part. He judged that in another minute the man would show himself. So believing, he laid his rifle across his stump, cocked it, and was ready to take aim and fire in a few seconds.

His foe's head appeared, after just about the delay that he had expected, and Robert's hand sprang to the trigger at the very moment the man pulled his own. The bullet hummed by his cheek. His finger contracted and then it loosened. A sudden acuteness of vision, or a chance thinning of the fog at that point, enabled him to see the man's face, and he recognized the French partisan, Charles Langlade, known also to the Indians as the Owl, who, with his wife, the Dove, had once held him in a captivity by no means unkind.

His humane instincts, his gratitude, his feeling for another flared up even in that moment of battle and passion, when the man-hunting impulse was so strong. His aim, quick as it was, had been sure and deadly, but, deflecting the muzzle of the rifle a shade, his finger contracted again. The spurt of fire leaped forth and the bullet sang by the ear of Langlade, singing to him a little song of caution as it passed, telling such a wary partisan as he that his stump was a very exposed stump, dangerous to the last degree, and that it would be better for him to find one somewhere else.

Robert did not see the Owl go away, but he was quite sure that he had gone, because it was just the sort of thing that such a skilled forest fighter would do. The fog thickened again, and, in a few more minutes, both lines shifted somewhat. Then he had to watch new stumps at new points, and his thoughts were once more in tune with those about him, concentrated on the battle and the man-hunt.

A bullet tipped his ear, and he saw that it came from a stump hardly visible in the fog. The sharpshooter was not likely to be Langlade again, and, at once, it became Robert's ambition to put him out of action. No consideration of mercy or humanity would restrain him now, if he obtained a chance of a good shot, and he waited patiently for it. Evidently this new sharpshooter had detected his presence also, and the second duel was on.

The man fired again in a minute or two, and the bullet chipped very close. He was so quick, too, that Robert did not get an opportunity to return his fire, but he recognized the face and to his great surprise saw that it was De Courcelles who had taken a place in line with the skirmishers. Rage seized him at once. This was the man who had tried to trick him to his death in that affair with the bully, Boucher, at Quebec. He was shaken with righteous anger. All the kindliness and mercy that he had felt toward Langlade disappeared. He was sure, too, that De Courcelles knew him and was trying his best to kill him.

Robert peered over his stump and sought eagerly for a shot. He could play at that game as well as De Courcelles, but his enemy was cautious. It was some time before he risked another bullet, and then Robert's, in reply, missed, though he also had been untouched. His anger increased. Although he had little hate in his composition he could not forget that this man De Courcelles had been a party to an infamous attempt upon his life, and even now, in what amounted to a duel, was seeking to kill him. His own impulses, under such a spur, and for the moment, were those of the slayer. He used all the skill that he had learned in the forest to secure an opportunity for the taking of his foe's life.

Robert sought to draw De Courcelles' fire again, meanwhile having reloaded his own rifle, and he raised his cap a little above the edge of the stump. But the trick was too old for the Frenchman and he did not yield to it. Taking the chance, he thrust up his face, dropping back immediately as De Courcelles' bullet sang over his head. Then he sprang up and was in time to pull trigger at his enemy, who fell back.

Robert was able to tell in the single glimpse through the fog that De Courcelles was not killed. The bullet had struck him in the shoulder, inflicting a wound, certainly painful but probably not dangerous, although it was likely to feed the man's hate of Robert. Even so, young Lennox was glad now that he had not killed him, that his death was not upon his hands; it was enough to disable him and to drive him out of the battle.

The fighting grew once more in volume and fury. Rifles cracked continuously up and down the line. The war whoop of the Indians was incessant, and the deep cheer of the borderers replied to it. But Robert saw that the end of the combat was near; not that the rage of man was abated, but because nature, as if tired of so much strife, was putting in between a veil that would hide the hostile forces from each other. The fog suddenly began to thicken rapidly, rolling up from the lake in great, white waves that made figures dim and shadowy, even a few paces away.

If the fighting went on it would be impossible to tell friend from foe, and Willet at once sent forth a sharp call which was repeated up and down the line. The French leaders took like action, and, by mutual consent, the two forces fell apart. The firing and the shouts ceased abruptly and a slow withdrawal was begun. The fog had conquered.

"Is Dagaeoga hurt?" asked Tayoga.

"Untouched," replied Robert.

"I saw that you and the Frenchman, De Courcelles, were engaged in a battle of your own. I might have helped you, but if I know you, you did not wish my aid."

"No, Tayoga. It was man to man. I confess that while our duel was on I was filled with rage against him, and tried my best to kill, but now I'm glad I gave him only a wound."

"Your hate flows away as De Courcelles' blood flows out."

"If you want to put it that way. But do you hear anything of the enemy, Tayoga? Fog seems to be a conductor of sound now and then."

"Nothing except the light noises of withdrawal. The retreating footsteps become fainter and fainter, and I think we shall have peace for to-day. They might fire bullets at random against the camp, but St. Luc will not let them waste lead in such a manner. No, Dagaeoga, we will lie quiet now and dress our wounds."

He was right, as the firing was not renewed, though the pickets, stationed at short intervals, kept as sharp a watch as they could in the fog, while the others lay by the fires which were now built higher than usual. Colden was hopeful that St. Luc would draw off, but Tayoga and Black Rifle, who went out again into the fog, reported no sign of it. Beyond a doubt, he was prepared to maintain a long siege.

"We must get help," said Willet. "We're supposed to control Lake George and we know that forces of ours are at the south end, where they've advanced since the taking of Fort William Henry. We'll have to send messengers."

"Who are they to be?" asked Colden.

"Robert and Tayoga are most fit. You have plenty of boats. They can take a light one and leave at once, while the fog holds."

Colden agreed. Young Lennox and the Onondaga were more than willing, and, in a half hour, everything was ready for the start. A strong canoe with paddles for two was chosen and they put in it their rifles, plenty of ammunition and some food.

"A year from now, if the war is still going on, I'll be going with you on such errands," said Grosvenor confidently.

"Red Coat speaks the truth. He learns fast," said Tayoga.

"I won't tell you lads to be careful, because you don't need any advice," said Willet.

Many were at the water's edge, when they pushed off, and Robert knew that they were followed by the best of wishes, not only for their success but for themselves also. A few strokes of the paddles and the whole camp, save a luminous glow through the fog, was gone. A few more strokes and the luminous glow too departed. The two were alone once more in the wilderness, and they had little but instinct to guide them in their perilous journey upon the waters. But they were not afraid. Robert, instead, felt a curious exaltation of the spirit. He was supremely confident that he and Tayoga would carry out their mission, in spite of everything.

"It is odd how quickly the camp sank from sight," he said.

"It is because we are in the heart of a great fog," said Tayoga. "Since it was thick enough to hide the battle it is thick enough also to hide the camp and us from each other. But, Dagaeoga, it is a friendly fog, as it conceals us from our enemies also."

"That's so, Tayoga, but I'm thinking this fog will hold dangers for us too. St. Luc is not likely to neglect the lake, and he'll surmise that we'll send for help. We've had experience on the water in fogs before, and you'll have to use your ears as you did then."

"So I will, Dagaeoga. Suppose we stop now, and listen."

But nothing of a hostile nature came to them through the mists and vapors, and, resuming the paddles again, they bore more toward the center of the lake, where they thought they would be likely to escape the cruising canoes of the enemy, if any should be sent out by St. Luc. They expected too that the fog would thin there, but it did not do so, seeming to spread over the full extent of Andiatarocte.

"How long do you think the fog will last?" asked Robert.

"All day, I fear," replied Tayoga.

"That's bad. If any of our friends should be on the shore we won't be able to see 'em."

"But we have to make the best of it, Dagaeoga. We may be able to hear them."

The fog was the greatest they had ever seen on Andiatarocte, seeming to ooze up from the depths of the waters, and to spread over everything. The keenest eyes, like those of Robert and Tayoga, could penetrate it only a few yards, and it hung in heavy, wet folds over their faces. It was difficult even to tell direction and they paddled very slowly in a direction that they surmised led to the south. After a while they stopped again that Tayoga might establish a new listening post upon the water, though nothing alarming yet came to those marvelous ears of his. But it was evident that he expected peril, and Robert also anticipated it.

"A force as large as St. Luc's is sure to have brought canoes overland," said young Lennox, "and in a fog like this he'll have them launched on the lake."

"It is so," said Tayoga, using his favorite expression, "and I think they will come soon."

They moved on once more a few hundred yards, and then, when the Onondaga listened a long time, he announced that the hostile canoes were on the lake, cruising about in the fog.

"I hear one to the right of us, another to the left, and several directly ahead," he said. "Sharp Sword brought plenty of canoes with him and he is using them. I think they have formed a line across the lake, surmising that we would send a message to the south. Sharp Sword is a great leader, and he forgets nothing."

"They can't draw a line that we won't pass."

Now they began to use their paddles very slowly and gently, the canoe barely creeping along, and Tayoga listening with all his powers. But the Onondaga was aware that his were not the only keen ears on the lake, and that, gentle as was the movement of the paddies that he and Robert held, it might be heard.

"The canoe on our right is coming in a little closer to us," he whispered. "It is a very large canoe, because it holds four paddles. I can trace the four separate sounds. They try to soften their strokes lest the hidden messenger whom they want to catch may hear them, but they cannot destroy the sound altogether. Now, the one on the left is bearing in toward us also. I think they have made a chain across the lake, and hope to keep anything from passing."

"Can you hear those ahead of us?"

"Very slightly, and only now and then, but it is enough to tell us that they are still there. But, Dagaeoga, we must go ahead even if they are before us; we cannot think of turning back."

"No such thought entered my head, Tayoga. We'll run this gauntlet."

"That was what I knew you would say. The canoes from both right and left still approach. I think they carry on a patrol in the fog, and move back and forth, always keeping in touch. Now, we must go forward a little, or they will be upon us, but be ever so gentle with the paddle, Dagaeoga. That is it! We make so little sound that it is no sound at all, and they cannot hear us. Now, we are well beyond them, and the two canoes are meeting in the fog. The men in them talk together. You hear them very well yourself, Dagaeoga. Their exact words do not come to our ears, but we know they are telling one another that no messenger from the beleaguered camp has yet passed. Now, they part and go back on their beat. We can afford to forget them, Dagaeoga, and think of those ahead. We still have the real gauntlet to run. Be very gentle with the paddle again.

"I hear the canoes ahead of us very clearly now. One of them is large also with four paddles in it, and two of the men are Frenchmen. I cannot understand what they say, but I hear the French accent; the sound is not at all like that the warriors make. One of the Frenchmen is giving instructions, as I can tell by his tone of command, and I think the canoes are going to spread out more. Yes, they are moving away to both right and left. They must feel sure that we are here somewhere in the fog, trying to get by them, but the big canoe with the Frenchmen in it keeps its place. Bear a little to the left, Dagaeoga, and we can pass it unseen."

It was the most delicate of tasks to paddle the canoe, and cause scarcely a ripple in the water, but they were so skillful they were able to do it, and make no sound that Robert himself could hear. Although his nerves were steady his excitement was intense. A situation so extraordinary put every power of his imagination into play. His fancy fairly peopled the water with hostile canoes; they were in a triple ring about him and Tayoga. All his pulses were beating hard, yet his will, as usual, was master of his nerves, and the hand that held the paddle never shook.

"A canoe on the outer line, and from the left, is now bearing in toward us," whispered Tayoga.

"There are two men in it, as the strokes of the paddles show. They are coming toward us. Some evil spirit must have whispered to them that we are here. Ah, they have stopped! What does it mean, Dagaeoga? Listen! Did you not hear a little splash? They think to surprise us! They keep the paddles silent and try a new trick! Hold the canoe here, Dagaeoga, and I will meet the warrior who comes!"

The Onondaga dropped his rifle, hunting shirt and belt with his pistol in it, into the bottom of the canoe, and then, his knife in his teeth, he was over the side so quickly that Robert did not have time to protest. In an instant he was gone in the fog, and the youth in the canoe could do nothing but wait, a prey to the most terrible apprehensions.

Robert, with an occasional motion of the paddle, held the canoe steady on the water, and tried to pierce the fog with his eyes. He knew that he must stay just where he was, or Tayoga, when he came back, might never find him. If he came back! If—He listened with all his ears for some sound, however slight, that might tell him what was happening.

Out of the fog came a faint splash, and then a sigh that was almost a groan. Young Lennox shuddered, and the hair on his head stood up a little. He knew that sound was made by a soul passing, but whose soul? Once more he realized to the full that his lot was cast in wild and perilous places.

A swimming face appeared in the fog, close to the canoe, and then his heart fell from his throat to its usual place. Tayoga climbed lightly into the canoe, no easy feat in such a situation, put on his belt and replaced the knife in the sheath. Robert asked him nothing, he had no need to do so. The sigh that was almost a groan had told the full tale.

"Now we will bear to the right again, Dagaeoga," said Tayoga, calmly, as the water dripped from him. Robert shivered once more. His fertile fancy reproduced that brief, fierce struggle in the water, but he said nothing, promptly following the suggestion of Tayoga, and sending the canoe to the right. The position was too perilous, though, for them to continue on one course long, and at the end of forty or fifty yards they stopped, both listening intently.

"Some of them are talking with one another now," whispered Tayoga. "The warrior who swam does not come back to his canoe, and they wonder why he stays in the water so long. Soon they will know that he is never coming out of the water. Now I hear a voice raised somewhat above the others. It is a French voice. It is not that of St. Luc, because he must remain on shore to direct his army. It is not that of De Courcelles, because you wounded him, and he must be lying in camp nursing his hurts. So I conclude that it is Jumonville, who is next in rank and who therefore would be likely to command on this important service. I am sure it is Jumonville, and his raised voice indicates that he is giving orders. He realizes that the swimmer will not return and that we must be near. Perhaps he knows or guesses that the messengers are you and I, because he has learned long since that we are fitted for just such service, and that we have done such deeds. For instance, our journey to Quebec, on which we first met him."

"Then he'll think Dave is here too, because he was with us then."

"No, he will be quite sure the Great Bear is not here. He knows that he is too important in the defense of the camp, that, while Captain Colden commands, it is the Great Bear who suggests and really directs everything. His sharp orders signify some sudden, new plan. They have a fleet of canoes, and I think they are making a chain, with the links connected so closely that we cannot pass. It is a real gauntlet for us to run, Dagaeoga."

"And how are we to run it?"

"We must pass as warriors, as men of their own."

"I do not look like a warrior."

"But you can make yourself look like one, in the fog at least, enough, perhaps, to go by. Your hair is a little long; take off your hunting shirt, and the other shirt beneath it, bare yourself to the waist, and in such a fog as this it would take the keenest of eyes, only a few yards away, to tell that you are white. Quick, Dagaeoga! Lay the garments on the bottom of the canoe. Bend well upon your paddle and appear to be searching the water everywhere for the messengers who try to escape. I will do the same. Ah, that is well. You look and act so much like a warrior of the woods, Dagaeoga, that even I, in the same canoe, could well take you for a Huron. Now we will whisper no more for a while, because they come, and they will soon be upon us."

Robert bent over his paddle. His upper clothing lay in the bottom of the canoe, with his rifle and Tayoga's upon the garments, ready to be snatched up in an instant, if need should come. The cold, wet fog beat upon his bare shoulders and chest, but he did not feel it. Instead his blood was hot in every vein, and the great pulses in his temples beat so hard that they made a roaring in his ears.

Distinct sounds now came from both left and right, the swish of paddles, the ripple of water against the side of a canoe, men talking. They were coming to the chain that had been stretched in front of them, and their fate would soon be decided. Now, they must be not only brave to the uttermost, but they must be consummate actors too.

Figures began to form themselves in the fog, the outline of a canoe with two men in it appeared on their right, another showed just ahead, and two more on the left. Robert from his lowered eyes, bent over the paddle, caught a glimpse of the one ahead, a great canoe, or rather boat, containing five men, one of whom wielded no paddle, but who sat in its center, issuing orders. Through the fog came a slight gleam of metal from his epaulets and belt, and, although the face was indistinct, Robert knew that it was Jumonville.

The officer was telling the canoes to keep close watch, not to let the chain be broken, that the messengers were close at hand, that they would soon be taken, and that their comrade who did not come back would be avenged. Robert bent a little lower over his paddle. His whole body prickled, and the roaring in his ears increased.

Tayoga suddenly struck him a smart blow across his bowed back, and spoke to him fiercely in harsh, guttural Huron. Robert did not understand the words, but they sounded like a stern rebuke for poor work with the paddle. The blow and the words stimulated him, keyed him to a supreme effort as an actor. All his histrionic temperament flared up at once. He made a poor stroke with the paddle, threw up much surplus water, and, as he cowered away from Tayoga, he corrected himself hastily. Tayoga uttered a sharp rebuke again, but did not strike a second time. That would have been too much. Robert's next stroke was fine and sweeping, and he heard Jumonville say in French which many of the Indians understood:

"Go more toward the center of the lake and take a place in the line."

Tayoga and Robert obeyed dumbly, passing Jumonville's boat at a range of five or six yards, going a little beyond the line, and, turning about as if to make a curve that would keep them from striking any other canoe. Again Robert made a false stroke with the paddle, causing the canoe to rock dangerously, and now, Tayoga, fully justified by the fierce code of the forest in striking him again, snatched his own paddle out of the water and gave him a smart rap with the flat of it across the back, at the same time upbraiding him fiercely in Huron.

"Dolt! Fool!" he exclaimed. "Will you never learn how to hold your paddle? Will you never know the stroke? Will you tip us both into the water at such a time, when the messengers of the enemy are seeking to steal through? Do better with the paddle or you shall stay at home with the old women, and work for the warriors!"

Robert snarled in reply, but he did not repay the blow. He made another awkward sweep that sent them farther on the outward curve, and he heard Jumonville's harsh laugh. He was still the superb actor. His excitement was real, and he counterfeited a nervousness and jerkiness that appeared real also. One more wild stroke, and they shot farther out. Jumonville angrily ordered them to return, but Robert seemed to be possessed by a spell of awkwardness, and Tayoga craftily aided him.

"Come back!" roared Jumonville.

Robert and Tayoga were fifteen yards away, and the great blanket of fog was enclosing them.

"Now! Now, Dagaeoga!" whispered the Onondaga tensely. "We paddle with all our might straight toward the south!"

Two paddles wielded by skillful and powerful arms flashed in the water, and the canoe sped on its way. A shout of anger rose behind them, and Robert distinctly heard Jumonville say in French:

"After them! After them! It was the messengers who stole by! They have tricked us!"

Those words were sweet in the ears of young Lennox. He had played the actor, and the reward, the saving of their lives, had been paid. It was one of their greatest triumphs and the savor of it would endure long. The very thought gave fresh power to his arm and back, and he swept his paddle with a strength that he had never known before. The canoe skimmed the water like a bird and fairly flew in their chosen course.

Robert's own faculties became marvelously acute. He heard behind them the repeated and angry orders of Jumonville, the hurried strokes of many paddles, the splashing of canoes turned quickly about, a hum of excited voices, and then he felt a great swell of confidence. The roaring in his ears was gone, his nerves became amazingly steady, and every stroke with his paddle was long and finished, a work of art.

Four or five minutes of such toil, and Tayoga rested on his paddle. Robert imitated him.

"Now we will take our ease and listen," said the Onondaga. "The fog is still our friend, and they will think we have turned to one side in it, because that is the natural thing to do. But you and I, Dagaeoga, will not turn just yet."

"I can't hear anything, Tayoga, can you?"

"I cannot, Dagaeoga, but we will not have long to wait. Now, I catch the light swish of a paddle. They are feeling about in the fog. There goes another paddle—and more. They come closer, but we still bide here a little. I hear the voice of Jumonville. He is very angry. But why should he be more angry at any other than at himself? He saw us with his own eyes. He shouts many sharp orders, and some of them are foolish. They must be so, because no man could shout orders so fast, and in such a confused way, and have them all good. He sends more canoes to both right and left to seek us. You and I can afford to laugh, Dagaeoga."

Sitting at rest in their canoe they laughed. With Robert it was not so much a laugh of amusement as a laugh of relief after such tremendous tension. He felt that they were now sure to escape, and with Tayoga he waited calmly.

CHAPTER XI.
THE HAPPY ESCAPE

The spirits of young Lennox rose to the zenith. Although they were still grazing the edge of peril, he had supreme confidence in Tayoga and also in the fog. It was a great fog, a thick fog, a kindly fog, and it had made possible their escape and the achievement of their mission. Having held so long it would hold until they needed it no longer.

"Have they come any nearer, Tayoga?" he asked.

"Jumonville is still giving orders, and sending the canoes somewhat at random. He is not the leader Sharp Sword would be in an emergency, nor anything like it. He is having his own boat paddled about uncertainly. I can hear the paddles of the four men in it. Now and then he speaks angrily, too. He is upbraiding those who are not to blame. How are you feeling now, Dagaeoga? Has Manitou already filled you with new strength?"

"I'm feeling as well as I ever did in my life. I'm ready to swing the paddle again."

"Then we go. The fog will not wait for us forever. We must use it while we have it."

They swept their paddles through the water in long and vigorous strokes, and the canoe shot forward once more. They were confident now that no enemy was ahead of them, and that none of those behind could overtake them. The wet, cold fog still enclosed them like a heavy, damp blanket, but their vigorous exercise and their high spirits kept them warm. After ten minutes they made another stop, but as Tayoga could hear nothing of Jumonville's party they pushed on again at speed. By and by the Onondaga said:

"I feel the fog thinning, Dagaeoga. A wind out of the west has risen, and soon it will take it all away."

"But it has served its purpose. I shall always feel well toward fogs. Yes, here it goes! The wind is rising fast, and it is taking away the mists and vapors in great folds."

The water began to roughen under the stiff breeze. The fog was split asunder, the pieces were torn to fragments and shreds, and then everything was swept away, leaving the surface of the lake a silver mirror, and the mountains high and green on either shore. Far behind them hovered the Indian canoes, and four or five miles ahead a tower of smoke rose from the west bank.

"Certainly our people," said Robert, looking at the smoke.

"There is no doubt of it," said the Onondaga, "and that is where we will go."

"And those behind us know now that we tricked them in the fog and have escaped. They give forth a shout of anger and disappointment. Now they turn back."

They eased their strokes a little as the pursuit had been abandoned, but curved more toward the center of the lake, lest some hidden sharpshooter on shore might reach them, and made fair speed toward the smoke, which Robert surmised might be made by a vanguard of troops.

"We ought to have help for Colden and Willet very soon," he said.

"It will not be long," said Tayoga; "but Dagaeoga has forgotten something. Can he not think what it is?"

"No, Tayoga, I can't recall anything."

"Dagaeoga's body is bare from the waist up. It is well for an Indian to go thus into a white camp, but it is not the custom of the people to whom Lennox belongs."

"You're right. I've had so much excitement that I'd forgotten all about my clothes. I must be true to my race, when I meet my brethren."

He reclothed himself, resumed his paddle, and they pushed on steadily for the smoke. No trace of the fog was left. The lake glistened in the sun, the ranges showed green from base to summit, and the tower of smoke deepened and broadened.

"Can you make out what lies at the foot of it, Tayoga?" asked Robert.

"I think I can see a gleam of the sun on an epaulet. It is certainly a camp of your people. The lake is supposed to be under their command, and if the French should make a new incursion here upon its shores they would not build their fires so boldly. Now, I see another gleam, and I hear the ring of axes. They are not boat builders, because no boats, either finished or unfinished, show at the water's edge. They are probably cutting wood for their fires. I hear, too, the crack of a whip, which means that they have wagons, and the presence of wagons indicates a large force. They may be coming ahead with supplies for our great army when it advances. I can now see men in uniform, and there are some red coats among them. Hold your paddle as high as you can, Dagaeoga, as a sign that we are friends, and I will send the canoe in toward the shore. Ah, they see us now, and men are coming down to the lake's edge to meet us! It is a large camp, and it should hold enough men to make St. Luc give up the siege of Colden."

The two sent the canoe swiftly toward the land, where soldiers and others in hunter's dress were already gathered to meet them. Robert saw a tall, thin officer in a Colonial uniform, standing on the narrow beach, and, assuming him to be in command, he said as the canoe swept in:

"We are messengers, sir, from the force of Captain Colden, which is besieged at the sawmill ten or twelve miles farther north."

"Besieged, did you say?" said the officer, speaking in a sharp, dry voice. "It's one of those French tricks they're always playing on us, rushing in under our very noses, and trying to cut out our forces."

"That's it, sir. The French and Indian host, in this case, is led by St. Luc, the ablest and most daring of all their partisans, and, unless you give help, they'll have to escape as best they can in what boats they have."

"As I'm a good Massachusetts man, I expected something of this kind. I sent word to Pownall, our Governor, that we must be extremely cautious in respect to the French, but he thinks the army of General Abercrombie will overwhelm everything. Forest fighting is very different from that of the open fields, a fact which the French seem to have mastered better than we have. My name, young sir, is Elihu Strong. I'm a colonel of the Massachusetts militia, and I command the force that you see posted here."

"And mine, sir, is Robert Lennox, a free lance, and this is Tayoga, of the clan of the Bear, of the great Onondaga nation, a devoted friend of ours and the finest trailer the world has ever produced."

"Ah, I heard something of you both when I was at Albany from one Jacobus Huysman, a stout and worthy burgher, who spoke well of you, and who hazarded a surmise that I might meet you somewhere in the neighborhood of the lakes."

"We lived in the house of Mynheer Jacobus when we went to school in Albany. We owe him much."

"There was a third who was generally with you, a famous hunter, David Willet, was there not?"

"He is with Captain Colden, sir, assisting in the defense."

"I'm glad he's there. Judging from what I've heard of him, he's a tower of strength. But come into the camp. Doubtless, both of you need food and rest. The times be dark, and we must get out of each day whatever it has to offer."

Robert looked at him with interest. He was the forerunner of a type that was to develop markedly in New England, tall, thin, dry-lipped, critical, shrewd and tenacious to the last degree. He and his kind were destined to make a great impress upon the New World. He gave to the two the best the camp had, and ordered that they be treated with every courtesy.

"I've a strong force here," he said, "although it might have been stronger if our Governor and Legislature had done their full duty. Still, we must make the best of everything. My men reported Indians in the forest to the north of us, and that, perhaps, is the reason why we have not come into contact with Captain Colden, but I did not suspect that he was besieged."

Robert, as he ate the good food set before him, looked over the camp, which had been pitched well, with far-flung pickets to guard against ambush, and his eyes glistened, as they fell upon two brass cannon, standing side by side upon a slight rise in the center of the camp. The big guns, when well handled, were always effective against forest warriors. Colonel Strong's eyes followed his.

"I see that you are taking notice of my cannon," he said. "They're good pieces, but if our governor and legislature had done their duty they'd be four instead of two. Still, we have to make the best of what we have. I told Shirley that we must prepare for a great war, and I tell Pownall the same. Those who don't know him always underrate our French foe."

"I never do, sir," said Robert. "I've seen too much of him to do that."

"Well, well, we'll do the best we can. I've four hundred men here, though if the Governor and the Legislature of Massachusetts had done their full duty they'd be eight hundred, not to say a thousand. I'll advance as soon as possible to the relief of Colden. He can surely hold out until the morrow."

"Not a doubt of it, sir, and, if you'll pardon me for making a suggestion, I wouldn't begin any advance until the morning. Not much of the day is left. If we started this afternoon, night would overtake us in the woods and the Chevalier de St. Luc is sure to plant an ambush for us."

"Sensibly spoken, young sir. We're an eternally rash people. We're always walking into traps. I've in my force about twenty good scouts, though if the Governor and Legislature of Massachusetts had done their full duty they'd be forty, not to say fifty, and I don't want to risk their loss in night fighting in the forest."

He went away and Robert saw him moving among his men, giving orders. Elihu Strong, a merchant, nevertheless had made himself a strenuous soldier at his province's call, and he was not unwilling to learn even from those not more than half his age.

"Open Eyes will do well," said Tayoga.

"Open Eyes?"

"Aye, Dagaeoga. The colonel who is named Strong I will call Open Eyes, because he is willing to look and see. He will look when you tell him to look, and many who come from the cities will not do that. And because his eyes are open he will not stick his head into an ambush. Yet he will always complain of others."

"And sometimes of himself, too," laughed Robert. "I think he'll be fair in that respect. Now, Tayoga, we'll rest here, and be easy with ourselves until to-morrow morning, when we advance."

"We will stay, Dagaeoga, but I do not know whether it will be so easy. Since Jumonville saw us escape he will tell St. Luc of it, and

Sharp Sword will send a force here to harry Open Eyes, and to make him think the forest is full of warriors. But Open Eyes, though he may complain, will not be afraid."

It was even as the Onondaga predicted. The foe came with the twilight. The dark wilderness about them gave back whoops and yells, and furtive bands skirmished with Strong's scouts. Then the shouts of the warriors increased greatly in number, and seemed to come from all points about the camp. It was obvious to Robert that the enemy was trying to make Strong's men believe that a great force was confronting them, and some of them, unused to the woods, showed apprehension lest such an unseen and elusive danger overwhelm them. But Elihu Strong never flinched. The forest was almost as much of a mystery to him as it was to his troops, but he was there to dare its perils and he dared them.

"I shall keep my men in camp and await attack, if they make it," he said to Robert, to whom he seemed to have taken a great fancy, "and whatever happens I shall move forward in the morning to the relief of Colden."

He shut his thin lips tightly together and his pale blue eyes flashed. The merchant, turned soldier, had the stoutest of hearts, and a stout heart was what was needed in his camp that night. The warriors gave his men no rest. They circled about continually, firing and whooping, and trying to create panic, or at least a fear that would hold Strong where he was.

Robert went to sleep early, and, when he awakened far in the night, the turmoil was still going on. But he saw Elihu Strong walking back and forth near one of the fires, and in the glow his thin face still reflected an iron resolution. Satisfied that the camp was in no danger of being frightened, young Lennox went back to sleep.

A gray, chilly morning came, and soon after dawn Elihu Strong began to prepare his men for their perilous progress, serving first an ample hot breakfast with plenty of tea and coffee.

"Open Eyes not only watches but he knows much," said Tayoga. "He has learned that an army marches better on a full stomach."

Strong then asked Robert and Tayoga to serve in a way as guides, and he made his dispositions, sending his scouts in advance, putting his most experienced soldiers on the flanks and heading his main column with the two brass cannon. The strictest injunctions that nobody straggle were given, and then the force took up its march.

They had not been molested while at breakfast, and when making the preparations, but as soon as they left the fire and entered the deep forest, the terrifying turmoil burst forth again, fierce whoops resounding on every side and bullets pattering on the leaves or bark. Colonel Strong left his scouts and flankers to deal with the ambushed warriors, and the main column, face to the front, marched steadily toward Colden's camp. It was to be a trial of nerves, and Robert was quite confident that the stern New England leader would win.

"The savages make a tremendous tumult," he said to young Lennox, "but their bullets are not reaching us. We're not to be shaken by mere noise."

"When they find that out, as they soon will," said Robert, "they'll make an attack. Some French officers and troops must be with them. Perhaps Jumonville came in the night to lead them."

He and Tayoga then went a short distance into the forest ahead of the scouts, and Tayoga saw ample evidence that the French were present with the Indians.

"You are right in your surmise that Jumonville came in the night," he said. "He wore boots, and here are the imprints of his heels. I think he is not far away now. Watch well, Dagaeoga, while I lie on the earth and listen."

Ear to the ground, the Onondaga announced that he could hear men on both sides of them moving.

"There is the light step of the warriors," he said, "and also the heavier tread of the French. I think I can hear Jumonville himself. It sounds like the crush of boots. Perhaps they are now seeking to lay an ambush."

"Then it's time for us to fall back, Tayoga, both for our own sakes and for the sake of Colonel Strong's force."

The two retreated quickly lest they be caught in an ambush, and gave warning to Elihu Strong that an attack was now probable, a belief in which they were confirmed by the report the scouts brought in presently that a creek was just ahead, a crossing always being a favorite place for an Indian trap.

"So be it," said Colonel Strong, calmly. "We are ready. If the Governor and Legislature of Massachusetts had done their full duty, we'd be twice as strong, but even as we are we'll force the passage of the creek."

"You will find a body of the warriors on this side of the stream," said Tayoga. "They will give way after a little firing, tempting you to think you have won an easy victory. Then when about half of your men are across they will attack with all their might, hoping to cut you down."

"I thank you for telling me," said Colonel Strong. "I've no doubt you know what you're talking about. Your manner indicates it. We might be much better equipped than we are if those in authority in my province had done their full duty, but we will make way, nevertheless. I'll cover the passage of the creek with the guns."

The firing in front already showed that Tayoga's prediction was coming true, and it was accompanied by a tremendous volume of yelling, as if the whole Indian force were gathered on the near side of the creek.

Robert from the crest of a hill saw the stream, narrow and deep, though not too deep for fording as he was to learn later, fringed on either side with a dense growth of low bushes, from the shelter of which warriors were sending their bullets toward the white force. The men were eager to go against them at once, but the scouts were sent forward through the undergrowth to open up a flanking fire, and then the main column marched on at a steady pace.

The crash of the rifles grew fast. The warriors on the near side of the creek leaped from the bushes as Strong's men drew near, waded the stream and disappeared in the forest on the other bank, giving forth howls of disappointment as they fled. The soldiers, uttering a shout of triumph, undertook to rush forward in pursuit, but Strong restrained them.

"It's the ambush against which the Onondaga warned us," he said to his lieutenants, "and we won't run into it. Bring forward the cannon."

The two brass guns, fine twelve pounders, were moved up within close range of the creek, and they swept the forest on the other side with balls and grape shot. It was probably the first time cannon were ever heard in those woods, and the reports came back in many echoes. Boughs and twigs rained down.

"It is a great sound," said Tayoga admiringly, "and the warriors who are trying to plant an ambush will not like it."

"But you'll remember Braddock's fate," said Robert. "The cannon didn't do much then."

"But this is different, Dagaeoga. Open Eyes has his eyes open. He is merely using the cannon as a cover for his advance. They will be backed up by the rifles. You will see."

The soldiers approached the creek cautiously, and, when the first ranks were in the water, the cannon raked the woods ahead to right and left, and to left and right. The best of the riflemen were also pushed forward, and, when the warriors opened fire, they were quickly driven away. Then the whole force, carrying the cannon with them, crossed, and stood in triumph on the other side.

"Did I not tell you that Open Eyes knew what he was doing?" said Tayoga.

"It seems that he does," Robert replied, "but we haven't yet arrived at Colden's station. An attack in force is sure to come."

"Dagaeoga speaks truth. I think it will occur a mile or two farther on. They will make it before Captain Colden's men can learn that we are on the march."

"Then they won't wait long. Anywhere will do, as the forest is dense everywhere."

Since they had carried the ford with but little loss, the cannon that had blazed the way ceased to fire, but the gunners regarded them proudly and Robert did not withhold admiration. They were pioneers, fine brass creatures, and when handled right they were a wonderful help in the forest. He did not blame the gunners for patting the barrels, for scraping the mud of the creek's crossing from the wheels, and for speaking to them affectionately. Massive and polished they gleamed in the sun and inspired confidence.

Tayoga went ahead in the forest, but came back soon and reported a low ridge not more than half a mile farther on, a likely place for an attack, which he judged would come there. It would be made by the united force of the French and Indians and would be severe.

"So be it," said Elihu Strong, whose iron calm nothing disturbed. "We are ready for the foe, though St. Luc himself should come. It is true that instead of two cannon we might have had four or even six, or twice as many men, if the Governor and Legislature of Massachusetts had done their full duty, but we'll let that pass. Will you, Lennox, and you, Tayoga, advance with the scouts and be my eyes?"

Robert appreciated the compliment to the full, and promptly replied in the affirmative for them both. Then he and Tayoga at once plunged into the forest with the borderers who were there to provide against ambush, all of them approaching the menacing ridge with great care. It was a long projection, rising about a hundred feet, and grown densely with trees and bushes. It looked very quiet and peaceful and birds even were singing there among the boughs. The leader of the scouts, a bronzed man of middle age named Adams, turned to Tayoga.

"I see nothing there," he said, "but I've heard of you and your power to find things where others can't. Do you think they're on that ridge waiting for us?"

"It is certain," replied the Onondaga. "It is the place best fitted for them, and they will not neglect it. Let me go forward a little, with my friend, Dagaeoga, and we will unveil them."

"We'll wait here, and if they're on it I believe you'll soon know it," said Adams confidently.

Tayoga slid forward among the bushes and Robert followed. Neither made the slightest noise, and they drew much nearer to the ridge, which still basked in the sun, peaceful and innocent in looks. Not a warrior or a Frenchman appeared there, the bushes gave back no glint of weapons, nothing was disclosed.

"They may be hidden in that jungle, but they won't stir until we're under the muzzles of their rifles. What do you propose to do?" asked Robert.

"I will tempt them, Dagaeoga."

"Tempt them? I don't understand you."

"Tododaho on his great star which we cannot see in the day, but which, nevertheless, is there, whispers to me that Tandakora himself is among the bushes on the ridge. It is just such an ambush as he loves. As you know, Dagaeoga, he hates us all, but he hates me most. If he sees a good opportunity for a shot at me he will not be able to forego it."

"For Heaven's sake, Tayoga, don't make a martyr of yourself merely to draw the enemy's fire!"

"No such thought was in my mind. I am not yet ready to leave the world, which I find bright and full of interest. Moreover, I wish to see the end of this war and what will happen afterward. Risks are a part of our life, Dagaeoga, but I will take none that is undue."

Tayoga spoke in his usual precise, book English, explaining everything fully, and Robert said nothing more. But he awaited the actions of the Onondaga with intense interest. Tayoga crept forward five or six yards more, and then he stumbled, striking against a bush and shaking it violently. Robert was amazed. It was incredible that the Onondaga should be so awkward, and then he remembered. Tayoga was going to draw the enemy's fire.

Tayoga struck against another bush, and then stood upright and visible. Those hidden on the ridge, if such there were, could see him clearly. The response was immediate. A gigantic figure stood up among the bushes, leveled a rifle and fired at him point blank. But the Onondaga, quick as lightning, dropped back and the bullet whistled over his head. Robert fired at the great painted figure of Tandakora, but he too missed, and in a moment the Ojibway chief sank down in the undergrowth. A shout came from the hidden Indians about him.

"They are there," said Tayoga, "and we know just where many of them lie. We will suggest to Open Eyes that he fire the cannon at that point."

They rejoined Adams.

"You were right, as I knew you'd be," said the scout. "You've located 'em."

"Yes, because Tandakora could not resist his hate of me," said the Onondaga.

They withdrew to the main force, and once more the brave brass guns were brought up, sending solid shot and grape into the bushes on the ridge, then moving forward and repeating the fire. Many rifles opened upon them from the thickets, and several men fell, but Elihu Strong held his people in hand, and the scouts drove back the sharpshooters. Meanwhile the whole force advanced and began to climb the ridge, the cannon being turned on the flanks, where the attack was now heaviest. A fierce battle ensued, and the guns, served with great skill and effectiveness, kept the Indians at bay. More of Strong's men were slain and many were hit, but their own rifles backed up the guns with a deadly fire. Thus the combat was waged in the thickets a full two hours, when they heard a great shout toward the north, and Willet, at the head of a hundred men, broke his way through to their relief. Then French and Indians drew off, and the united forces proceeded to the point, where Colden, Wilton, Carson and Grosvenor gave them a great welcome.

"We are here," said Elihu Strong. "If the Governor and Legislature of Massachusetts had done their full duty we might have been here sooner, but here we are."

"I knew that you would come back and bring help with you," said Grosvenor to Robert. "I felt sure that Tayoga would guide the canoe through every peril."

"Your confidence was not misplaced," said Robert. "He did some wonderful work. He was as great a trailer on the water as he is on land. Now that we are so much stronger, I wonder what St. Luc is going to do."

But Black Rifle came in the next morning with the news that the Chevalier and his whole force were gone.

They had stolen away silently in the night, and were now marching northward, probably to join Montcalm.

"I'm not surprised," said Willet. "We're now too strong for him and St. Luc is not the man to waste his time and strength in vain endeavors. I suspect that we will next hear of him near Champlain, somewhere in the neighborhood of Ticonderoga. I think we'd better follow his trail a little distance."

Willet himself led the band that pursued St. Luc, and it included Tayoga, Robert, Grosvenor, Black Rifle and Adams, Daganoweda and his Mohawks having left shortly before on an expedition of their own. It was an easy enough task, as the trail necessarily was wide and deep, and the Onondaga could read it almost with his eyes shut.

"Here went Sharp Sword," he said after looking about a while. "I find traces of his moccasins, which I would know anywhere because I have seen them so many times before. Here another Frenchman joined him and walked beside him for a while. It was Jumonville, whose imprints I also know. They talked together. Perhaps Jumonville was narrating the details of his encounter with us. Now he leaves St. Luc, who is joined by another Frenchman wearing moccasins. But the man is heavy and walked with a heavy step. It is the Canadian, Dubois, who attends upon Sharp Sword, and who is devoted to him. Perhaps Sharp Sword is giving him instructions about the camp that they will make when the day is over. Now Dubois also goes, and here come the great moccasins of Tandakora. I have seen none other so large in the woods, and a child would know them. He too talks with Sharp Sword, but Sharp Sword does not stop for him. They walk on together, because the stride continues steady and even, just the length that a man of Sharp Sword's height would make when walking. Tandakora is very angry, not at Sharp Sword—he would not dare to show anger against him—but at the will of Manitou who would not let him win a victory over us. He did not get much satisfaction from Sharp Sword, because he stayed with him only a very short time. Here his trail leads away again, and Sharp Sword once more walks on alone.

"Perhaps Sharp Sword prefers to be alone. Most men do after a disappointment, and he knows that his attack upon the boat builders has been a failure. Sharp Sword does not like failures any more than other people do, and he wants to think. He is planning how to win a great success, and to atone for his failure here. I do not see anything of De Courcelles. I do not find his trail anywhere, which shows that the wound you gave him, Dagaeoga, was severe. He is being carried either by warriors or French soldiers on a litter. It is far more likely to be soldiers, and here I find them, the trail of four men who walk exactly even, two by two all the time. The rage of De Courcelles will mount very high against you, Dagaeoga, and you will have to beware of him."

"I am ready for him," said Robert, proudly.

The broad trail led steadily on toward the north, but Willet, after a while, spread out his own little force, taking no chances with forest ambush. He considered it highly probable that before long Tandakora would curve aside with some of his warriors, hoping to trap the unwary. He was confirmed in his opinion by the Onondaga's reading of the trail.

"I find the footprints of the Ojibway chief again," said Tayoga. "Here they go at the edge of the trail. Now he has stopped. His stride has ceased, and he stands with his moccasins close together. He is probably talking with his warriors and he meditates something. The rage of Tandakora is as great as that of De Courcelles, but Tandakora is not hurt, and he is able to strike. He moves on again, and, ah! here he goes into the woods. Beyond question he is now engaged in planting an ambush for those who would follow St. Luc. Shall we go back, Great Bear, or shall we meet the Ojibway's ambush with an ambush of our own?"

The black eyes of the Onondaga sparkled.

"We ought to turn back," replied Willet, "but I can't resist playing Tandakora's own game with him. It may give us a chance to rid the border of that scourge. We'll leave the trail, and go into the deep bush."

Led by the hunter the little band plunged into the forest and began a careful circle, intending to come back to the trail some distance ahead, and to post themselves behind Tandakora in case that wily savage was planning an ambush, as they felt sure he was. They redoubled their precautions, ceasing all talk for the while, and allowing no bushes to rustle as they passed. Willet led the line, and Tayoga brought up the rear. Grosvenor was just behind Robert. He, too, was now able to bring down his feet in soundless fashion, and to avoid every stick or twig that might break with a crack beneath his weight. While he was aware of the perils before them, his heart beat high. He felt that he was making further progress, and that he was becoming a worthy forest runner.

After two careful hours of travel, they came back again to the broad trail which showed that St. Luc was still maintaining steady progress toward the north. But both the hunter and the Onondaga felt sure that Tandakora and a chosen band were now to the south, waiting in ambush for those who would come in pursuit.

"We'd better draw 'em if we can," said Willet. "Let 'em know we're here, but make 'em believe we're friends."

"I think I can do it," said Tayoga. "I know Huron and St. Regis signals. It is likely that some of the warriors with Tandakora are Hurons, and, in any event, the Ojibway will understand the signals."

He imitated the cawing of a crow, and presently the answer came from the forest about a quarter of a mile to the south. The cry was repeated, and the answer came duly a second time. No one in the little band now doubted that Tandakora and his men were there.

"Shall we attack?" asked Robert.

"I think we can sting them a little," replied Willet. "Our numbers are few, but the force of the Ojibway is not likely to be large. It was his purpose to strike and get away, and that's what we'll do. Now, Tayoga, we're relying upon you to get us into a good position on his flank."

The Onondaga led them in another but much smaller circle toward the forest, from which the answering caws of the crow had come. The way went through dense thickets but, before he reached his chosen spot, he stopped.

"Look," he said, pointing to the earth, where there were faint traces that Robert could scarcely see and over which he would have passed, unnoticing. "Here is where Tandakora went on his way to the ambush. It is a little trail, and it was to be only a little ambush. He has only about ten warriors with him. The Ojibway has come back for revenge. He could not bear to leave without striking at least one blow. Perhaps he slipped away from Sharp Sword to try the ambush on his own account."

"They can't be far ahead," said the hunter.

"No," said the Onondaga. "They will be coming back in response to my call, and I think we would better await them here."

They disposed themselves in good order for battle, and then sank to the earth. Light waves of air registered delicately but clearly on those wonderful eardrums of Tayoga's. Faint though the sound was, he understood it. It was the careful tread of men. Tandakora and his warriors were on the way, called by the crow. He knew when they came within a hundred yards of where he and his companions lay, and he knew when they spread out in cautious fashion, to see what manner of friends these were who came. He knew, too, that Tandakora would not walk into a trap, and he had not expected at any time that he would, it having been merely his purpose when he cawed like a crow to call him back to fair and honorable combat, ambush against ambush. He noted when the thin line of detached warriors began to advance again, he was even able to trace the step of Tandakora, heavier than the others, and to discern when the Ojibway chief stopped a second time, trying to pierce the thickets with his eyes.

"Tandakora is in doubt," he whispered to Robert. "The call of the crow which at first seemed so friendly has another meaning now. He is not so sure that friends are here after all, but he does not understand how an enemy happens to be behind him. He is angry, too, that his own pretty ambush, in which he was sitting so cunningly waiting for us, is broken up. Tandakora's humor is far from good, but, because of it, mine is excellent."

"You certainly learned the dictionary well when you were in our schools," Robert whispered back, but as full as ever of admiration for Tayoga's powers. "Has all sound ceased now?"

"They are not stirring. They have become quite sure that we are enemies and they wait for us to act first."

"Then I'll give 'em a lead," said Willet, who lay on Tayoga's right.

He thrust out a foot, bringing it down on a dead stick so hard that it broke with a sharp snap, but instantly drew away to the shelter of another bush. A rifle cracked in front of them and a bullet cut the air over the broken stick. Before the warrior who fired the bullet could sink back Black Rifle pulled the trigger at a certain target, and the man fell without a sound.

"A fine shot, Captain Jack," said Willet, and a few minutes later the hunter himself made another just as good. For a half hour the combat was waged in the deep thickets, mere glimpses serving for aim, but the combatants were as fierce and tenacious as if the issue were joined by great armies. Four warriors fell, Willet's band suffered only a few scratches, and then, at a signal from him, they melted away into the woods, curved about again, and took up the return journey toward their own force.

"We did enough," said Willet, when he was sure they were not pursued by Tandakora. "All we wanted to do was to sting the Ojibway and not to let him forget that those who ambush may be ambushed. He'll be fairly burning with anger."

"How are you feeling, Red Coat?" asked Tayoga.

"As well as could be expected after such an experience," replied Grosvenor with pride. But the young Englishman was very sober, too. A warrior had fallen before his rifle, and, with the heat of battle over, he was very thoughtful.

CHAPTER XII.
THE FRENCH CAMP

They returned to the camp without further event. Colden and Strong were gratified to learn that the retreat of St. Luc was real, and that he was certainly going toward Champlain, with the obvious intention of joining Montcalm.

"We owe you a great debt of gratitude, Colonel," said the young officer, frankly, to Elihu Strong. "If you had not come I don't think we could have held out against St. Luc."

"We did the best we could," replied Elihu Strong. "If the Governor and Legislature of Massachusetts had done their full duty we'd have been here earlier, with twice as many men and guns, but as it is we did our best, and man can do no more."

They decided that they would hold the point and await the coming of the great army under Abercrombie which was to crush Montcalm. The outworks were built higher and stronger and the brass cannon were mounted upon them at points, where they could sweep the forest. These fine twelve-pounders were sources of much moral courage and added greatly to the spirits of the troops. They had shown their power at the forcing of the ford and at the taking of the ridge, and their brazen mouths, menacing the forest, looked well.

Willet and his comrades considered it their duty to stay there also, and wait for Abercrombie, and, the third day after the retreat of St. Luc, Robert and Tayoga went into the woods to see whether Tandakora had turned back again with his warriors. They reckoned that the Ojibway chief's anger was so strong that he would make another attempt at revenge upon those who had defeated him. There was a rumor that the Indians with the French were becoming much dissatisfied, that they were awed by the reports of the mighty British and American force advancing under Abercrombie, and might leave the French to meet it alone.

"Do you think there is much in these rumors?" asked Robert, as he and the Onondaga went into the forest.

"I do," replied Tayoga. "The warriors with the French do not like the cannon, and they say the force that is coming against Montcalm is very vast. A great battle may be fought, but Tandakora and his men are not likely to be there. They will go away and await a better day."

"Then I'm glad they'll desert for a while. They're the eyes and ears of the French. That will leave our own scouts and forest runners the lords of the wild, though it seems to me, Tayoga, that you're the true and veritable lord of the wild."

"Then if that were so, though you praise my skill too much, Dagaeoga, you and the Great Bear and Black Rifle also are lords of the wild."

"Lords of the wild! I like the term. It is something to be that at this time and in this region. We're mainly a wilderness people, Tayoga, and our wars are waged in the woods. We're not more than two miles from the camp now, and yet we're completely lost in the forest. There's not a trace of man. I don't even see any smoke soiling the sky."

"It is so, Dagaeoga, and we are again in the shadow of peril. Dangers in the forest are as thick as leaves on the trees. Here is an old trail of our enemies."

"I'm not interested in old trails. What we're looking for is new ones."

"If we keep going toward the north it may be that we will find them, Dagaeoga."

Several miles farther on they came to other trails which the Onondaga examined with great interest and care. Two or three he pronounced quite recent, but he did not read any particular purpose in them.

"It is likely that they were made by hunters," he said. "While the armies are gathering, the warriors are sure to seek game. Here two of them passed, and here they stood behind a tree. It is sure now that those two were hunting. I think they stood behind a tree to ambush a deer. The deer was to the west of them. The traces they left in the soft earth under the tree show that the toes of their moccasins pointed toward the west and so they were looking that way, at the deer, which probably stood in the thicket over there nibbling at its food. They must have had an easy shot. Now, we'll enter the thicket. Lo, Dagaeoga, here is where the deer fell! Look at the little bushes broken and at the dark stain on the ground where its life flowed out. They dragged the body to the other side of the thicket, and cut it up there. Nothing could be plainer, the traces are so numerous. They were casual hunters, and it is not worth our while to follow them."

Northward they still pursued their course, and struck another and larger trail which made Tayoga look grave.

"This is the path of seven or eight warriors," he said, "and it is likely that they are a scouting party. They have come back, as we expected, to spy upon us and to cut off stragglers from our camp. We will follow it a little while."

It led south by west and seemed to go on with a definite purpose, but, after a mile or so, it divided, four warriors, as Tayoga said, going in one direction and three in the other.

"Suppose I follow those on the north a short distance while you take those on the south," suggested Robert.

"We will do so," said Tayoga, "and in an hour come back to this point."

The three warriors were on the north, and, as the earth was soft, Robert saw their trail quite clearly leading steadily west by north. His own ambition to excel as a trailer was aroused and he followed it with great energy. Two or three times when the ground became hard and rocky he lost it, but a little search always disclosed it again, and he renewed the pursuit with increased zeal. He went on over a hill and then into a wide valley, well grown with thickets. Pushing his way through the bushes he sought the traces and was startled by a sound almost at his shoulder. Keyed to the dangers of the forest he whirled instantly, but it was too late. A powerful warrior threw himself upon him, and though Robert, by a great effort, threw him off he sprang back and another on the other side also seized him. He was borne to the earth and a third Indian coming up, he was quickly secured.

Robert at first was so sick with chagrin that he did not think about his life. In nine cases out of ten the warriors would have tomahawked him, and this he soon realized, thankful at the same time that he had been spared, for the present, at least. Yet his mortification endured. What would Tayoga say when he saw by the trail that he had been caught so easily? He had fairly walked into the trap, and he was now a prisoner the second time. Yet he showed the stoicism that he had learned in a forest life. While the Indians bound his wrists tightly with rawhide thongs he stood up and looked them squarely in the face.

One of the warriors took his rifle and examined it with a pleased eye. Another appropriated his pistol and a third helped himself to his knife and hatchet.

"I've four shillings in an inside pocket," said Robert. "If you want 'em, take 'em."

But the warriors did not understand English and shook their heads. Evidently they were satisfied with the spoil they had taken already.

"Which way?" asked Robert.

They replied by leading him to the northwest. He was hopeful at first that Tayoga might rescue him as he had done once before, but the warriors were wary and powerful, and three, too, were too many for the Onondaga alone to attack. The thought passed and by an effort of the will he resigned himself to his immediate captivity. They did not mean to take his life, and while there was no hope for the present there was plenty of it for the future. He could be in a far worse case. His unfailing optimism broke through the shell of mortification, and he became resolutely cheerful.

"Which way, my friends?" he said to the warriors.

But again they understood no English and shook their heads.

"Don't plume yourself too much on that rifle," he said, speaking to the warrior who had taken his favorite weapon. "You have it for the present, but when I escape for the second time I mean to take it with me. I give you fair warning."

The warrior, who seemed to be good natured, shook his head once more, and grinned, not abating at all his air of proprietorship so far as the rifle was concerned.

"And you with the pistol," continued the prisoner, "I beg to tell you it's mine, not yours, and I shall claim it again. What, you don't understand? Well, I'll have to find some way to make you comprehend later on."

The three warriors walked briskly and Robert, of course, had no choice but to keep pace with them. They indicated very conclusively that they knew where they meant to go, and so he assumed that a hostile camp was not very far away. Resolved to show no sign of discouragement, he held his head erect and stepped springily.

About three miles, and he saw a gleam of uniforms through the trees, a few steps more and his heart gave a leap. He beheld a group of Indians, and several Frenchmen, and one of them, tall, young, distinguished, was St. Luc.

The Chevalier was in a white uniform, trimmed with silver, a silver hilted small sword by his side, and his smile was not unpleasant when he said to Robert:

"I sent out these three warriors to find me a prisoner and bring him in, but I little suspected that it would be you."

"I suspected as little that it was you to whom I was being taken," said Robert. "But since I had to be a prisoner I'm glad I'm yours instead of De Courcelles' or Jumonville's, as those two soldiers of France have as little cause to love me as I have to love them."

"Monsieur De Courcelles is suffering from a bullet wound."

"It was my bullet."

"You say that rather proudly, but perhaps I'd better not tell it to him. It seems, Mr. Lennox, that you have a certain facility in getting yourself captured, as this is the second time within a year."

"I was treated so well by the French that I thought I could risk it again," said Robert jauntily.

The Chevalier smiled. Robert felt again that current of understanding and sympathy, that, so it seemed to him, had passed so often between them.

"I see," said St. Luc, "that you are willing to give credit to France, the evergreen nation, the nation of light and eternal life. We may lose at times, we may be defeated at times, but we always rise anew. You British and Americans will realize that some day."

"I do not hate France."

"I don't think you do. But this is scarcely a time for me to give you a lecture on French qualities. Sit down on this log. I trust that my warriors did not treat you with undue harshness."

"I've nothing to complain of. They took my weapons, but that is the law of war. I'd have done the same in their place. As I see it, they're not particularly bad Indians. But if you don't mind, I'd like you to cut these rawhide thongs that bind my wrists. They're beginning to sting."

The Chevalier drew a knife and with one sweep of its keen edge severed the rawhide. Robert's wrists flew apart and the blood once more flowed freely through his veins. Though the stinging did not cease he felt great relief.

"I thank you," he said politely, "but, as I told you before, I do not hold it against your warriors, because they bound me. I'd have escaped had they given me any chance at all, and I warn you now, as I warned them, that I intend to escape later on."

St. Luc smiled.

"I'll accept the challenge," he said, "and I'll see that you don't make good your boast. I can assure you, too, if by any possibility you should escape, it certainly will not be before the great battle."

"Great battle! What great battle? You don't mean that Montcalm will dare to meet Abercrombie?"

"Such an idea was in my mind."

"Why, we'll come with four or five to one! The Marquis de Montcalm cannot stand against such a powerful force as ours. We've definite information that he won't be able to muster more than three or four thousand men. We hear, too, that the Indians, frightened by our power, are leaving him, for the time, at least."

"Some of your surmises may be correct, but your facts don't follow from them. The Marquis de Montcalm, our great leader, will await your Abercrombie, no matter what your force may be. I violate no military secret when I tell you that, and I tell you also that you are very far from being assured of any victory."

The Chevalier suddenly dropped his light manner, and became intensely earnest. His eyes gleamed for an instant with blue fire, but it was only a passing moment of emotion. He was in an instant his old, easy self again.

"We talk like the debaters of the schools," he said, "when we are at war. I am to march in a few minutes. I suggest that in return for certain liberties you give me your pledge to attempt no escape until we arrive at the camp of the Marquis de Montcalm."

"I can't do it. Since I've promised you that I will escape I must neglect no chance."

"So be it. Then I must guard you well, but I will not have your wrists bound again. Here comes an expert rover of the forest who will be your immediate jailer."

A white man at the head of several warriors was approaching through the woods. He was young, lean, with a fierce, hooked Roman nose, and a bold, aggressive face, tanned to the color of mahogany. Robert recognized him at once, and since he had to be a prisoner a second time, he took a certain pleasure in the meeting.

"How do you do, Monsieur Langlade?" he said. "You see, I've come back. I forgot to tell you good-by, and I'm here to make amends for my lack of politeness. And how is the patient and watchful spouse, the Dove?"

Robert spoke in good French and the partisan stared in astonishment. Then a pleased look of recognition came into his eyes.

"Ah, it's young Mr. Lennox," he exclaimed. "Young Mr. Lennox come back to us. It's not mere politeness that makes me tell you I'm glad to see you. You did make a very clever escape with the aid of that Indian friend of yours. I hope to capture Tayoga some day, and, if I do, it will be an achievement of which I shall boast all the rest of my life. But we'll take good care that you don't leave us again."

"He has just warned me that he intends to escape a second time," said St. Luc.

"Then it will be a pretty test of mettle," said the Owl, appreciation showing in his tone, "and we welcome it. Have you any commands for me, sir?"

He spoke with great respect when he addressed the query to St. Luc, and the Chevalier replied that they would march in a half hour. Then Langlade gave Robert food, and took a little himself, sitting with the prisoner and informing him that the Dove had worried greatly over his escape. Although she was not to blame, she considered that in some indirect manner it was a reflection upon her vigilance, and it was many months before she was fully consoled.

"I must send word to her by one of our runners that you have been retaken," said the Owl, "and I wish to tell you, Mr. Lennox, that the Dove's younger sister, who is so much like her in looks and character, is still unmarried and perhaps it may come into the mind of the Chevalier de St. Luc or the Marquis de Montcalm to send you back to our village."

"You're once more most polite," laughed Robert, "but I'm far too young, yet, to think of marriage."

"It's not an offer that I'd make to many young men," said Langlade regretfully. "In truth, I know of none other to whom I'd have mentioned it."

When they took up the march the force numbered about fifty men, and Robert walked between Langlade and a stalwart Indian. St. Luc was further on. They did not seem to fear any ambush and Langlade chattered after his fashion. He made the most of the French resources. He spoke as if the Marquis de Montcalm had ten or fifteen thousand veteran French regulars, and half as many Indian warriors.

"Don't consider me contentious, Monsieur Langlade," said Robert, at last, "but I know full well that your general has not half that many troops, no, not a third, and that nearly all his Indians are about to leave him."

"And how do you know that?" exclaimed the Owl. "Well, one Frenchman equals two of the English or the Bostonnais, and that doubles our numbers. You don't see any chance to escape, do you?"

"Not at present," laughed Robert.

"Not now, nor at any other time. No man ever escapes twice from the French."

The talk of Langlade, his frank egotism and boastfulness for himself personally and for the French collectively, beguiled the journey which soon became strenuous, the force advancing at a great pace through the forest. At night a fire was built in the deep woods, the knapsacks furnished plenty of food, and Robert slept soundly on a blanket until dawn. He had seen before closing his eyes that a strict guard was set, and he knew that it was not worth while to keep awake in the hope of escape. Like a wise man he dismissed the hope of the impossible at once, and waited calmly for another time. He knew too that St. Luc had originally sent out his warriors to capture a prisoner from whom they might drag information, but that the Chevalier would not try to cross-examine him, knowing its futility.

They traveled northward by east all the next day, through very rough country, slept another night in the forest, and on the third day approached a great camp, which held the main French force. Robert's heart thrilled. Here was the center of the French power in North America. Vaudreuil and Bigot at Quebec might plan and plot and weave their webs, but in the end the mighty struggle between French and English and their colonies must be decided by the armies.

He knew that this was the outlet of Lake George and he knew also that the army of Abercrombie was gathering at the head of the same lake. His interest grew keener as they drew nearer. He saw clusters of tents, cannon parked, and many fires. There were no earthworks or other fortifications, and he inferred from their absence that Montcalm was undecided whether to go or stay. But Robert thought proudly that he would surely go, when the invincible Anglo-American army advanced from its base at the head of the lake. The whole camp lay under his eye, and he had enough military experience now to judge the French numbers by its size. He did not think they were much in excess of three thousand, and as Abercrombie would come four or five to one, Montcalm must surely retreat.

"I take it that this is Ticonderoga," he said to St. Luc.

"Aye," replied the Chevalier.

"And in effect you have Champlain on one side of you and George on the other. But you can't hold the place against our great force. I'm here in time to join you in your retreat."

"We don't seem to be retreating, as you'll notice, Mr. Lennox, and I don't know that we will. Still, that rests on the knees of the gods. I think you'll find here some old friends and enemies of yours, and though your people have made a great outcry against the Marquis de Montcalm because of the affair at Fort William Henry, I am sure you will find that the French know how to treat a prisoner. I shall put you for the present in the care of Monsieur Langlade, with whom you appear to have no quarrel. He has his instructions."

It was the second time that Robert had entered the camp of Montcalm and his keen interest drove away for the present all thought of himself. He noted anew the uniforms, mostly white faced with blue or violet or red or yellow, and with black, three-cornered hats. There were the battalions of Guienne, La Reine, Béarn, La Sarre,

Languedoc, Berry and Royal Roussillon. The Canadians, swarthy, thick and strong, wore white with black facings. Some Indians were about, but fewer than Robert had expected. It was true then that they had become alarmed at Abercrombie's advancing might, and were leaving the French to their fate.

"You are to stay in a tent with me," said Langlade, "and you will be so thoroughly surrounded by the army, that you will have no earthly chance of escape. So I think it better that you pledge your word not to attempt it for a while, and I can make things easier for you."

"No, I decline again to give such a pledge," said Robert firmly. "I warn you, as I've warned the Chevalier de St. Luc, that I'm going to escape."

Langlade looked at him searchingly, and then the face of the partisan kindled.

"I believe you mean it!" he exclaimed. "You rely on yourself and you think, too, that clever Onondaga, Tayoga, will come again to your aid. I acknowledge that he's a great trailer, that he's master of some things that even I, Charles Langlade, the Owl, do not know, but he cannot steal you away a second time."

"I admit that I've been thinking of Tayoga. He may be here now close to us."

The Owl gave a startled look at the empty air, as if he expected Tayoga to be hovering there, formidable but invisible. ·

"I see you do fear him," laughed Robert.

"I do, but we shall be a match for him this time, though I never underrate his powers."

A young officer in a captain's uniform stopped suddenly and looked at Robert. Then he advanced and extended his hand.

"It is evident that you like the French," he said, "since you are continually coming back to them."

"De Galissonnière!" exclaimed Robert, as he warmly shook the extended hand. "Yes, here I am, and I do like many of the French. I'm sorry we're official enemies."

"I know that our people will treat you well," jested De Galissonnière, "and then, when we take New York, you can tell the inhabitants of that city what good masters we are and teach them to be reconciled."

Young Lennox made a reply in like spirit, and De Galissonnière passed on. But a man walking near with his shoulder well bound greeted him in no such friendly manner. Instead a heavy frown came over his face and his eyes flashed cruelly. It was De Courcelles, nursing the wound Robert had given him, and at the same time increasing his anger. The youth returned his gaze defiantly.

"Colonel De Courcelles does not like you," said Langlade, who had noticed the brief exchange.

"He does not," replied Robert. "It was my bullet that hurt his shoulder, but I gave him the wound in fair combat."

"And he hates you because of it?"

"That and other things."

"What a strange man! A wound received in fair and honorable battle should be a tie that binds. If you had given it to me in a combat on equal terms I'd have considered it an honor conferred upon me by you. It would have wiped away all grievance and have made us friends."

"Then, Monsieur Langlade, I'm afraid I missed my opportunity to make our friendship warmer than it is."

"How is that?"

"I held you also under the muzzle of my rifle in that battle in the forest, but when I recognized you I could not send the bullet. I turned the weapon aside."

"Ah, that was in truth a most worthy and chivalrous act! Embrace me, my friend!"

"No! No! We American men never embrace or kiss one another!"

"I should have remembered. A cold people! But never mind! You are my brother, and I esteem you so highly that I shall let nothing on earth take you away from us. Can you not reconsider your decision about the sister of the Dove? She would make you a most admirable wife, and after the war we could become the greatest rangers, you and I, that the forest has ever known. And the life in the woods is marvelous in its freedom and variety!"

But Robert plead extreme youth once more, and the Owl was forced to be resigned. The small tent in which guard and prisoner were to sleep was almost in the center of the camp and Robert truly would have needed wings and the power of invisibility to escape then. Instead of it he let the thought pass for a while and went to sleep on a blanket.

* * * * *

While young Lennox slept St. Luc was in the tent of Montcalm talking with his leader. The Marquis was in much perplexity. His spies had brought him word of the great force that was mustering in the south, and he did not know whether to await the attack at Ticonderoga or to retreat to the powerful fortifications at Crown Point on Lake Champlain. His own ardent soul, flushed by the successes he had already won, told him to stay, but prudence bade him go. Now he wanted to hear what St. Luc had to say and wanting it he knew also that the Chevalier was the most valiant and daring of his captains. He wished to hear from the dauntless leader just what he wished to hear and nothing else.

"Your observations, then, confirm what the spies have reported?" he said. "The enemy can easily control Lake George!"

"He has only to make an effort to do so, my general," replied St. Luc. "I could have captured the boat builders on the point or have compelled their retirement, but large forces came to their relief. The numbers of the foe are even greater than we had feared."

"How many men do you think General Abercrombie will have when he advances against us?"

"Not less than fifteen thousand, sir, perhaps more."

The face of Montcalm fell.

"As many as that!" he exclaimed. "It is more than four to one!"

"He cannot have less, sir," repeated St. Luc positively.

Montcalm's brow clouded and he paced back and forth.

"And the Indians who have been so powerful an ally," he said at last. "They are frightened by the reports concerning the Anglo-American army. After their fashion they wish to run away before superior force, and fight when the odds are not so great. It is most embarrassing to lose their help, at such a critical time. Can you do nothing with this sullen giant, Tandakora, who has such influence over them?"

"I fear not, sir. He was with me on the expedition from which I have just returned, and he fared ill. He is in a most savage humor. He is like a bear that will hide in the woods and lick its hurts until the sting has passed. I think we may consider it certain, sir, that they will desert us, for the time."

"And we shall have but little more than three thousand French and Canadians to defend the honor of France and His Majesty's great colony in North America. We might retreat to the fortifications at Crown Point, and make an advantageous stand there, but it goes ill with me to withdraw. Still, prudence cries upon me to do so. I have talked with Bourlamaque, Trepezec, Lotbiniére, the engineer, Langy, the partisan, and other of my lieutenants whom you know. They express varying opinions. Now, Colonel de St. Luc, I want yours, an opinion that is absolutely your own."

St. Luc drew himself up and his warrior soul flashed through his blue eyes.

"Sir," he said, "it goes as ill with me as it does with you to retreat. My heart is here at Ticonderoga. Nor does prudence suggest to me that we retreat to Crown Point. My head agreeing with my heart says that we should stand here."

"And that is your conviction?"

"It is, sir. Ticonderoga is ours and we can keep it."

"Upon what do you base this opinion? In such a crisis as this we must be influenced by sound military reasons and not by sentiment."

"My reasons, sir, are military. That is why my heart goes with my head. It is true that the Anglo-American army will come in overwhelming numbers, but they may be overwhelming numbers that will not overwhelm. As we know, the British commanders have not adapted themselves as well as the French to wilderness, campaigning. Their tactics and strategy are the same as those they practice in the open fields of Europe, and it puts them at a great disadvantage. We have been willing to learn from the Indians, who have practiced forest warfare for centuries. And the British Colonials, the Bostonnais, fall into the faults of the parent country. In spite of all experience they, continue to despise wilderness wile and stratagem, and in a manner that is amazing. They walk continually into ambush, and are cut up before they can get out of it. I am not one to cheapen the valor of British and British Colonials. It has been proved too often on desperate fields, but in the kind of war we must wage here deep in the wilds of North America, valor is often unavailing, and I think, sir, that we can rely upon one fact. The enemy will take us too lightly. He is sure to do something that will keep him from using his whole force at the right moment against us. Our forest knowledge will work all the time in our behalf. I entreat you, sir, to keep the army here at Ticonderoga and await the attack."

St. Luc spoke with intense earnestness, and his words had all the ring of conviction. Montcalm's dark face was illumined. Again he walked back and forth, in deep thought.

"The engineer, Lotbiniére, a man whose opinion I respect, is of your mind," he said at last. "He says that whether Crown Point or Ticonderoga, it's merely either horn of the dilemma, and naturally, if the dangers of the two places are even, we prefer Ticonderoga and no retreat. The Marquis de Vaudreuil had a plan to save Ticonderoga by means of a diversion with a heavy force under Bourlamaque, De Levis and Longueuil into the Mohawk Valley. But some American rangers taken near Lake George by Langy told him that Abercrombie already had thirty thousand men at the head of George and the Marquis at once abandoned the scheme. It was lucky for us the rangers exaggerated so much that the plan was destined to failure, as we needed here the men who were sent on it. We save or lose Ticonderoga by fighting at Ticonderoga itself and by nothing else. I thank you, Colonel de St. Luc, for your gallant and timely words, I have been wavering and they have decided me. We stay here and await the Anglo-American army."

"And the star of France will not fail us," said St Luc, with intense conviction.

"I trust not. I feel more confidence since I have decided, and I do know this: the young men who are my lieutenants are as brave and skillful leaders as any chief could desire. And the troops will fight even ten to one, if I ask it of them. It is a pleasure and a glory to command troops of such incomparable bravery as the French. But we must try to keep the Indians with us. I confess that I know little about dealing with them. Has this savage chief, Tandakora, come back to Ticonderoga?"

"I think he is here, sir. Do you wish me to talk with him?"

"I do. I wish it very much."

"He is very sullen, sir. He holds that the Indians have received no rewards for their services."

"We have given them blankets and food and muskets and ammunition."

"He takes those as a matter of course. But he means something else. To tell you the truth, sir, the savages want us to give prisoners to them."

Montcalm's face clouded again.

"To burn at the stake, or to torture to death otherwise!" he exclaimed. "My reputation and what is more, the reputation of France, suffers already from the massacre at William Henry, though God knows I would have prevented it if I could. It happened so suddenly and so unexpectedly that I could not stop it, until the harm was done. But never, St. Luc, never will I give up a prisoner to them for their tortures, though every savage in our armies desert us!"

"I hold with you, sir, that we cannot surrender prisoners to them, even though the cause of France should suffer."

"Then talk to this savage chief. Make him see reason. Promise him and his people what you wish in muskets, ammunition, blankets and such things, but no prisoners, not one."

St. Luc, with a respectful salute, left the tent. He was torn by conflicting emotions. He was depressed over the smallness of the French numbers, and yet he was elated by Montcalm's decision to stay at Ticonderoga and await Abercrombie. He was confident, as he had said, that some lucky chance would happen, and that the overwhelming superiority of the Anglo-American army would be nullified.

The Chevalier cast a discriminating eye over the French position. The staunch battalion of Berry lay near the foot of Lake George, but the greater part of the army under the direct command of Montcalm was in camp near a saw mill. The valiant Bourlamaque was at the head of the portage, and another force held the point of embarkation on Lake George. But he knew that Montcalm would change these dispositions when the day of battle came.

On the westward side of the camp several fires burned and dark figures lay near them. St. Luc marked one of these, a gigantic savage, stretched at his ease, and he walked toward him. He pretended, at first, that his errand had nothing to do with Tandakora, but stood thoughtfully by the fire, for a minute or two. Nor did the Ojibway chief take any notice. He lay at ease, and it was impossible to tell what thoughts were hidden behind his sullen face.

"Does Tandakora know what the commander of the French army has decided to do?" said St. Luc, at last.

"Tandakora is not thinking much about it," replied the chief.

"Montcalm is a brave general. He shows that he is not afraid of the great army the English and the Bostonnais have gathered. He will not retreat to Crown Point or anywhere else, but will stay at Ticonderoga and defeat his foes."

The black eyes of the Ojibway flickered.

"Tandakora does not undertake to tell Montcalm what he must do," he said, "nor must Montcalm undertake to tell Tandakora what he should do. What Montcalm may do will not now keep Tandakora awake."

St. Luc's heart filled with hot anger, but he was used to dealing with Indians. He understood their minds from the inside, and he had a superb self-control of his own.

"We know that Tandakora is a great chief," he said evenly. "We know too that he and his men are as free as the winds. As they blow where they please so the warriors of Tandakora go where they wish. But Onontio [The Governor-General of Canada.] and Tandakora have long been friends. They have been allies, they have fought side by side in many a battle. If Onontio falls, Tandakora falls with him. If the British and Bostonnais are victorious, there will be room for none of the tribes save the League of the Hodenosaunee, and them Tandakora hates. Onontio will not be able to protect them any more, and they will be driven from all their hunting grounds."

He paused to watch his words take effect and they obviously stirred the soul of the savage chief who moved uneasily.

"It is true," he said. "Sharp Sword never tells a falsehood. If Onontio is struck down then the British, the Bostonnais and the Hodenosaunee triumph, but my warriors bring me word that our enemies have gathered the greatest force the world has ever seen at the head of Andiatarocte. They come thicker than the leaves of the forest. They have more guns than we can count. They will trample Montcalm and his soldiers under their feet. So, according to our custom, Tandakora and his warriors would go away into the forest, until the British and the Bostonnais scatter, unable to find us. Then, when they are not looking, we will strike them and take many scalps."

Tandakora spoke in his most impressive manner, and, when he ceased, his eyes met St. Luc's defiantly. Again the blood of the Chevalier burned with wrath, but as before he restrained himself, and his smooth voice gave no hint of anger as he replied:

"Odds are of no avail against Montcalm. The children of Onontio are used to dealing with them. Remember, Tandakora, the great victories Montcalm won at Oswego and William Henry. He has the soul of a mighty chief. He has decided to stay here at Ticonderoga and await the enemy, confident that he will win the victory. Tandakora is a great warrior, is he willing to have no share in such a triumph?"

The cruel eyes of the Ojibway glistened.

"The heart of Tandakora is heavy within him," he said. "He and his warriors are not afraid of the British and the Bostonnais. They have fought by the side of Montcalm, but they do not receive all the rewards that Onontio owes them."

"Onontio has given to them freely of his muskets and powder and bullets, and of his blankets and food."

"But he takes from them the prisoners. We have no scalps to carry home."

"It is against the custom of the French to put prisoners to death or torture. Moreover, we have no prisoners here. The rangers taken by Langy have already been sent to Canada."

"There is one in the camp now. He was captured by three of my warriors, those you sent out, and by the law of war he belongs to me. Yet Sharp Sword and Montcalm hold him. I speak of the youth Lennox, the comrade of the Onondaga, Tayoga, who is my bitterest enemy. I hate Lennox too because he has stood so often in my way and I demand him, to do with as I please, because it is my right."

The Ojibway moved close to St. Luc and the fierce black eyes glared into those of stern blue. The Chevalier did not change his smooth, placatory tone as he replied:

"I cannot give up Lennox. It is true that he was taken by your warriors, but they were then in my service, so he is my prisoner. But he is only a single captive, a lad. Ask for some other and greater reward, Tandakora, and it shall be yours."

"Give me the prisoner, Lennox, and I and my warriors stay and fight with you at Ticonderoga. Refuse him and we go."

The chief's words were sharp and decisive and St. Luc understood him. He knew that the savage Ojibway hated young Lennox intensely, and would put him to the torture. He never hesitated an instant.

"I cannot yield the prisoner to you," he said. "The custom of the French will not permit it."

"The warriors are a great help in battle, and the reward I ask is but small. St. Luc knows that Montcalm needs men here. What is this boy to St. Luc that he refuses so great a price for him?"

"It cannot be done, Tandakora. I keep the prisoner, Lennox, and later I will send him to Canada to be held there until the war is over."

"Then the forest to-morrow will swallow up Tandakora and his warriors."

The chief returned to the fire and lay at ease in his blanket. St. Luc walked thoughtfully back toward the tent of Montcalm. He knew that it was his duty to report the offer of Tandakora to his chief, but he did so reluctantly.

"You have refused it already?" said the Marquis.

"I have, sir," replied St. Luc.

"Then you have done well. I confirm you in the refusal."

St. Luc saluted with great respect, and again retired from the tent.

CHAPTER XIII.
EVE OF BATTLE

Robert awoke the next morning, well physically, but depressed mentally. He believed that a great battle—and a great victory for the Anglo-American army—was coming, and he would have no part in it. The losses of Braddock's defeat and the taking of Fort William Henry by Montcalm would be repaired, once more the flag of his native land and of his ancestral land, would be triumphant, but he would be merely a spectator, even if he were as much as that. It was a bitter reflection, and again he thought of escape. But no plan seemed possible. He was held as firmly in the center of an army, as if he were in the jaws of a powerful vise. Nor was it possible for Tayoga, however great his skill and daring, to reach him there. He strove to be philosophical, but it is hard for youth to reconcile itself at first, though it may soon forget.

Breakfast was given to him, and he was permitted to go outside the tent into a small open space, though not beyond. On all sides of him stretched the impassable lines of the French army. There were several other prisoners within the enclosure, a ranger, a hunter, and three or four farmers who had been taken in forays farther south.

The fresh air and the brilliant sunshine revived Robert's spirits. He looked eagerly about him, striving to divine the French intentions, but he could make nothing of them. He knew, however, upon reflection, that this would be so. The French would not put any prisoners in a position to obtain information that would be of great value in the possible event of escape.

He undertook to talk with the other prisoners, but they were a melancholy lot, not to be cheered. They were all thinking of a long, in truth, an indefinite, imprisonment in Canada, and they mourned. Many people had been taken into Canada by French and Indians in former forays and had been lost forever.

Robert turned away from his comrades and sat down on a stone, where he speculated idly on what was passing about him. He believed that the French would withdraw to Crown Point, at least, and might retreat all the way to Canada, leaving Lake Champlain, as well as Lake George, to the complete control of the Anglo-American forces. He expected to see preparations to that effect, and, when he saw none, he concluded that they were merely postponed for a day or two. So far as he could judge, the aspect of the French army was leisurely. He did not observe any signs of trepidation, but then, withdrawal was always easy in the great North American wilderness. There was yet plenty of time for it.

He noticed a complete absence of Indians, and the fact struck him with great surprise. While he was advancing various theories to account for it, young Captain Louis de Galissonnière came, and greeted him cordially.

"I hope you understand that we French know how to treat a prisoner," he said.

"I've nothing of which to complain," replied Robert. "This is the second time that I've been with you, and on this occasion, as on the first, I seem to be more of a guest than a captive."

"You're the special prisoner of Colonel de St. Luc, who stands extremely high with the Marquis de Montcalm. The colonel wishes you to be treated well and seems to favor you. Why is it?"

"Frankly, I don't know, but I learned long since that he was a most chivalrous foe. I suppose I am to be sent into Canada along with the other prisoners?"

"I suppose so, but there is no way for you to go just now."

"Why can't I go with your army?"

"With our army?"

"It retreats, of course, before our overwhelming force."

De Galissonnière laughed.

"You are disposed to be facetious," he said. "You will observe that we are not retreating. You see no preparations to do so, but that's all I will tell you. More would be valuable information for the enemy, should you escape."

"I've warned Colonel de St. Luc that I mean to escape in due time. I don't like to reject such noble hospitality as you're showing me, but my duty to my country demands it."

Robert was now in a most excellent humor. His sanguine temperament was asserting itself to the full. What he wished to see he saw. He was slipping away from the French; and he was advancing with the English and Americans to a great and brilliant victory. His face was flushed and his eyes sparkled. De Galissonnière looked at him curiously, but said nothing.

"I observe one very significant fact," continued Robert.

"What is that?"

"I see no Indians, who are usually so numerous about your camps. You needn't tell me what has happened, but I've been among Indians a great deal. I know their ways, and I'll tell you. They see that yours is a lost cause, and they've deserted you. Now, isn't that so?"

The young Frenchman was silent, but it was the turn of his face to flush.

"I didn't expect you to answer me in words," continued Robert, triumphantly, "but I can see. The Indians never fight in a battle that they consider lost before it's joined, and you know as well as I do, Captain de Galissonnière, that if the Marquis de Montcalm awaits our attack his army will be destroyed."

"I do not know it at all."

Then Robert felt ashamed because he had been led away by his enthusiasm, and apologized for a speech that might have seemed boastful to the young Frenchman, who had been so kind to him. But De Galissonnière, with his accustomed courtesy, said it was nothing, and when he left, presently, both were in the best of humors.

Robert, convinced that he had been right about the Indians, watched for them as the morning went on, but he never saw a single warrior. There could be no doubt now that they had gone, and while he could not consider them chivalric they were at least wise.

The next familiar face that he beheld was one far from welcome to him. It was that of a man who happened to pass near the enclosure and who stopped suddenly when he caught sight of Robert. He was in civilian dress, but he was none other than Achille Garay, that spy whose secret message had been wrested from him in the forest by Robert and Tayoga.

The gaze that Garay bent upon Robert was baleful. His capture by the three and the manner in which he had been compelled to disclose the letter had been humiliating, and Robert did not doubt that the man would seek revenge. He shivered a little, feeling that as a prisoner he was in a measure helpless. Then his back stiffened.

"I'm glad to see, Garay, that you're where you belong—with the French," he called out. "I hope you didn't suffer any more from hunger in the woods when Willet, the Onondaga and I let you go."

The spy came closer, and his look was so full of venom that young Lennox, despite himself, shuddered.

"Time makes all things even," he said. "I don't forget how you and your friends held me in your power in the forest, but here you are a prisoner. I have a good chance to make the score even."

Robert remembered also how this man had attempted his life in Albany, for some reason that he could not yet fathom, and he felt that he was now, and, in very truth, a most dangerous enemy. Nevertheless, he replied, quietly:

"That was an act of war. You were carrying a message for the enemy. We were wholly within our rights when we forced you to disclose the paper."

"It makes no difference," said Garay. "I owe you and your comrades a debt and I shall pay it."

Robert turned his back on him and walked to the other side of the enclosure. When he turned around, five minutes later, Garay was gone. But Robert felt uncomfortable. Here was a man who did not have the gallantry and chivalry that marked so many of the French. If he could he would strike some great blow.

He strove to dismiss Garay from his mind, and, in his interest in what was going on about him, he finally succeeded. He saw Frenchmen and Canadians leaving the camp and others returning. His knowledge of war made him believe that those coming had been messengers sent forth to watch the Anglo-American army, and those going were dispatched on the same service. Their alarm must be great, he reflected pleasantly, and none could bring to Montcalm any reassuring news. Once he saw Montcalm, and once St. Luc, but neither spoke to him.

He and his comrades, the other prisoners, slept that night in the open, the weather being warm. A blanket was allotted to every one by their captors, and Robert, long used to unlimited fresh air, preferred the outside to the inside of a tent. Nothing disturbed his slumbers, but he expected that the French retreat would begin the next day. On the contrary, Montcalm stayed in his camp, nor was there any sign of withdrawal on the second and third days, or on others that came. He inferred then that the advance of Abercrombie had been delayed, and the French were merely hanging on until their retreat became compulsory.

He had been in the camp about a week, and as he saw no more of Garay he concluded that the man had been sent away on some errand. It was highly probable that he was now in the south spying upon the Anglo-American army. It was for just such duties that he was fitted. Then he began to think of him less and less.

His old impatience and keen disappointment because he was a prisoner when such great days were coming, returned with doubled vigor. He chafed greatly and looked around again for an opportunity to escape, but did not see the remotest possibility of it. After all, he must reconcile himself. His situation could be far worse. He was well treated, and some of the French leaders, while official enemies, were personal friends.

His mind also dwelled upon the singular fact that the French army did not retreat. He tried to glean something from De Galissonnière, who talked with him several times, but the young captain would not depart from generalities. He invariably shut up, tight, when they approached any detail of the present military situation.

A dark night came with much wind and threat of rain. Robert thought that he and his fellow captives would have to ask the shelter of tents, but the rain passed farther to the west, though the heavy darkness remained. He was glad, as the weather was now oppressively warm, and he greatly preferred to sleep on a blanket in the open air.

The night was somewhat advanced when he lay down. The other prisoners were asleep already. He had not found any kindred minds among them, and, as they were apathetic, he had not talked with them much. Now, he did not miss them at all as he lay on his blanket and watched the wavering lights of the camp. It was still quite dark, with a moaning wind, but his experience of weather told him that the chance of rain was gone. Far in the west, lightning flickered and low thunder grumbled there now and then, but in the camp everything was dry. Owing to the warmth, the fires used for cooking had been permitted to burn out, and the whole army seemed at peace.

Robert himself shared this feeling of rest. The storm, passing so far away, soothed and lulled him. It was pleasant to lie there, unharmed, and witness its course at a far point. He dozed a while, fell asleep, and awoke again in half an hour. Nothing had changed. There was still an occasional flicker of lightning and mutter of thunder and the darkness remained heavy. He could dimly see the forms of his comrades lying on their blankets. Not one of them stirred. They slept heavily and he rather envied them. They had little imagination, and, when one was in bad case, he was lucky to be without it.

The figure lying nearest him he took to be that of the hunter, a taciturn man who talked least of them all, and again Robert felt envy because he could lose all care so thoroughly and so easily in sleep. The man was as still and unconcerned as one of the mountain peaks that looked down upon them. He would imitate him, and although sleep might be unwilling, he would conquer it. A resolute mind could triumph over anything.

He shut his eyes and his will was so strong that he held them shut a full ten minutes, although sleep did not come. When he opened them again he thought that the hunter had moved a little. After all, the man was mortal, and had human emotions. He was not an absolute log.

"Tilden!" he called—Tilden was the hunter's name.

But Tilden did not stir, nor did he respond in any way when he called a second time. He had been mistaken. He had given the man too much credit. He was really a log, a dull, apathetic fellow to whom the extraordinary conditions around them made no appeal. He would not speak to him again as long as they were prisoners together, and, closing his eyes anew, he resolutely wooed slumber once more.

Robert's hearing was not so wonderfully keen as Tayoga's, but it was very keen, nevertheless, and as he lay, eyes shut, something impinged upon the drums of his ears. It was faint, but it did not seem to be a part of the usual sounds of the night. His ear at once registered an alarm on his brain.

His eyes opened. The man whom he had taken to be the hunter was bending over him, and, dark though it was, he distinctly saw the gleam of a knife in his hand. His first feeling, passing in a flash, was one of vague wonderment that anybody should menace him in such a manner, and then he saw the lowering face of Garay. He had been a fool to forget him. With a convulsive and powerful effort he threw his body to one side, and, when the knife fell, the blade missed him by an inch.

Then Robert sprang to his feet, but Garay, uttering an angry exclamation at his missed stroke, did not attempt another. Instead, agile as a cat, he ran lightly away, and disappeared in the darkness of the camp. Robert sat down, somewhat dazed. It had all been an affair of a minute, and it was hard for him to persuade himself that it was real. His comrades still slept soundly, and the camp seemed as peaceful as ever.

For a time Robert could not decide what to do. He knew that he had been threatened by a formidable danger, and that instinct, more than anything else, had saved him. He was almost prepared to believe that Tayoga's Tododaho, looking down from his remote star, had intervened in his behalf.

The question solved itself. Although he knew that Garay had made a foul attempt upon his life he had no proof. His story would seem highly improbable. Moreover, he was a prisoner, while Garay was one of the French. Nobody would believe his tale. He must keep quiet and watch. He was glad to see that the night was now lightening. Garay would not come back then, at least. But Robert was sure that he would repeat the attack some time or other. Revenge was a powerful motive, and he undoubtedly had another as strong. He must guard against Garay with all his five senses.

The night continued to brighten. The lightning ceased to flicker, the storm had blown itself out in the distance, and a fine moon and a myriad of stars came out. Things in the camp became clearly visible, and, feeling that Garay would attempt nothing more at such a time, Robert closed his eyes again. He soon slept, and did not awaken until all the other prisoners were up.

"Mr. Tilden," he said to the hunter, "I offer you my sincere apologies."

"Apologies," said the hunter in surprise. "What for?"

"Because I mistook a much worse man for you. You didn't know anything about it at the time, but I did it, and I'm sorry I wronged you so much, even in thought."

The hunter touched his forehead. Clearly the misfortunes of the young prisoner were weighing too heavily upon him. One must endure captivity better than that.

"Don't take it so hard, Mr. Lennox," he said. "It's not like being in the hands of the Indians, and there is always the chance of escape."

De Galissonnière visited him again that morning, and Robert, true to his resolution, said nothing of Garay. The captain did not speak of the Anglo-American army, but Robert judged from his manner that he was highly expectant. Surely, Abercrombie was about to advance, and the retreat of Montcalm could not be more than a day away. De Galissonnière stayed only ten minutes, and then Robert was left to his own devices. He tried to talk to Tilden, but the hunter lapsed again into an apathetic state, and, having little success, he fell back on his own thoughts and what his eyes might behold.

In the afternoon he saw Montcalm at some distance, talking with St. Luc and Bourlamaque, and then he saw a man whose appearance betokened haste and anxiety approach them. Robert did not know it then, but it was the able and daring French partisan, Langy, and he came out of the forest with vital news.

* * * * *

Meanwhile Langy saluted Montcalm with the great respect that his successes had won from all the French. When the Marquis turned his keen eye upon him he knew at once that his message, whatever it might be, was of supreme importance.

"What is it, Monsieur Langy?"

"A report on the movements of the enemy."

"Come to my tent and tell me of it fully, and do you, St. Luc and Bourlamaque, come with me also. You should hear everything."

They went into the tent and all sat down. St. Luc's eyes never left the partisan, Langy. He saw that the man was full of his news, eager to tell it, and was impressed with its importance. He knew Langy even better than Montcalm did. Few were more skillful in the forest, and he had a true sense of proportion that did not desert him under stress. His eyes traveled over the partisan's attire, and there his own great skill as a ranger told him much. His garments were disarranged. Burrs and one or two little twigs were clinging to them. Obviously he had come far and in haste. The thoughts of St. Luc, and, in truth, the thoughts of all of them, went to the Anglo-American army.

"Speak, Monsieur Langy," said Montcalm. "I can see that you have come swiftly, and you would not come so without due cause."

"I wish to report to you, sir," said Langy, "that the entire army of the enemy is now embarked on the Lake of the Holy Sacrament, and is advancing against us."

Montcalm's eyes sparkled. His warlike soul leaped up at the thought of speedy battle that was being offered. A flame was lighted also in St. Luc's blood, and Bourlamaque was no less eager. It was no lack of valor and enterprise that caused the French to lose their colonies in North America.

"You know this positively?" asked the commander-in-chief.

"I have seen it with my own eyes."

"Tell it as you saw it."

"I lay in the woods above the lake with my men, and I saw the British and Americans go into their boats, a vast flock of them. They are all afloat on the lake at this moment, and are coming against us."

"Could you make a fair estimate of their numbers?"

"I obtained the figures with much exactitude from one or two stragglers that we captured on the land. My eyes confirm these figures. There are about seven thousand of the English regulars, and about nine thousand of the American colonials."

"So many as that! Five to one!"

"You tell us they are all in boats," said St. Luc. "How many of these boats contain their artillery?"

"They have not yet embarked the cannon. As nearly as we can gather, the guns will not come until the army is at Ticonderoga."

"What?"

"It is as I tell you," replied Langy to St. Luc. "The guns cannot come up the lake until a day or two after the army is landed. Their force is so great that they do not seem to think they will need the artillery."

St. Luc, his face glowing, turned to Montcalm.

"Sir," he said, "I made to you the prophecy that some chance, some glorious chance, would yet help us, and that chance has come. Their very strength has betrayed them into an error that may prove fatal. Despising us, they give us our opportunity. No matter how great the odds, we can hold earthworks and abattis against them, unless they bring cannon, or, at least we may make a great attempt at it."

The swarthy face of Montcalm was illumined by the light from his eyes.

"I verily believe that your gallant soul speaks truth, Chevalier de St. Luc!" he exclaimed. "I said once that we would stand and I say it again. We'll put all to the hazard. Since they come without cannon we do have our chance. Go, Langy, and take your needed rest. You have served us well. And now we'll have the others here and talk over our preparations."

The engineers Lotbiniére and Le Mercier were, as before, zealous for battle at Ticonderoga, and their opinion counted for much with Montcalm. De Levis, held back by the vacillating Vaudreuil, had not yet come from Montreal, and the swiftest of the Canadian paddlers was sent down Lake Ticonderoga in a canoe to hurry him on. Then the entire battalion of Berry went to work at once with spade and pick and ax to prepare a breastwork and abattis, stretching a line of defense in front of the fort, and not using the fort itself.

* * * * *

Robert saw the Frenchmen attack the trees with their axes and the earth with their spades, and he divined at once the news that Langy had brought. The Anglo-American army was advancing. His heart throbbed. Victory and rescue were at hand.

"Mr. Tilden," he said to the hunter, "listen to the ring of the ax and the thud of the spade!"

"Aye, I hear 'em," was the apathetic reply; "but they don't interest me. I'm a prisoner."

"But it may mean that you won't be a prisoner much longer. The French are fortifying, and they've gone to work with so much haste and energy that it shows an imminent need. There's only one conclusion to be drawn from it. They're expecting our army and a prompt attack."

Tilden began to show interest.

"On my life, I think you're right," he said.

And yet Montcalm changed his mind again at the last moment. Two veteran officers, Montguy and Bernès, pointed out to him that his present position was dominated by the adjacent heights, and in order to escape that danger he resolved to retreat a little. He broke up his camp late in the afternoon of the next day, part of the army fell back through the woods more than a mile, and the rest of it withdrew in boats on the lake to the same point.

Robert and his comrades were carried with the army on land to the fort. There he became separated from the others, and remained in the rear, but luckily for his wishes, on a mount where he could see most that was passing, though his chance of escape was as remote as ever.

He stood on the rocky peninsula of Ticonderoga. Behind him the great lake, Champlain, stretched far into north and south. To the west the ground sloped gently upward a half mile and then sank again. On each side of the ridge formed thus was low ground, and the ridge presented itself at once to the military eye as a line of defense. Hugues, one of his officers, had already recommended it to Montcalm, and men under two of his engineers, Desandrouin and Pontleroy, were now at work there.

The final line of defense was begun at dawn, and Robert, whom no one disturbed, witnessed a scene of prodigious energy. The whole French army threw itself heart and soul into the task. The men, hot under the July sun, threw aside their coats, and the officers, putting their own hands to the work, did likewise. There was a continuous ring of axes, and the air resounded with the crash of trees falling in hundreds and thousands.

The tops and ends of the boughs were cut off the trees, the ends left thus were sharpened and the trees were piled upon one another with the sharp ends facing the enemy who was to come.

Robert watched as these bristling rows grew to a height of at least nine feet, and then he saw the men build on the inner side platforms on which they could stand and fire over the crest, without exposing anything except their heads. In front of the abattis more trees with sharpened boughs were spread for a wide space, the whole field with its stumps and trees, looking as if a mighty hurricane had swept over it.

Robert was soldier enough to see what a formidable obstruction was being raised, but he thought the powerful artillery of the attacking army would sweep it away or level it. He did not know that the big guns were being left behind. In truth, Langy's first news that the cannon would not be embarked upon the lake was partly wrong. The loading of the cannon was delayed, but after the British and Americans reached their landing and began the march across country for the attack, the guns, although brought down the lake, were left behind as not needed. But the French knew all these movements, and whether the cannon were left at one point or another, it was just the same to them, so long as they were not used in the assault.

Robert's intense mortification that he should be compelled to lie idle and witness the efforts of his enemies returned, but no matter how he chafed he could see no way out of it. Then his absorption in what was going on about him made him forget his personal fortunes.

The setting for the great drama was wild and picturesque in the extreme. On one side stretched the long, gleaming lake, a lake of wildness and beauty associated with so much of romance and peril in American story. Over them towered the crest of the peak later known as Defiance. To the south and west was Lake George, the Iroquois Andiatarocte, that gem of the east, and, on all sides, save Champlain, circled the forest, just beginning to wither under the fierce summer sun.

The energy of the French did not diminish. Stronger and stronger grew abattis and breastwork, the whole becoming a formidable field over which men might charge to death. But Robert only smiled to himself. Abercrombie's mighty array of cannon would smash everything and then the brave infantry, charging through the gaps, would destroy the French army. The French, he knew, were brave and skillful, but their doom was sure. Once St. Luc spoke to him. The chevalier had thrown off his coat also, and he had swung an ax with the best.

"I am sorry, Mr. Lennox," he said, "that we have not had time to send you away, but as you can see, our operations are somewhat hurried. Chance put you here, and here you will have to stay until all is over."

"I see that you are expecting an army," said Robert, "and I infer from all these preparations that it will soon be upon you."

"It is betraying no military secret to admit that it is even so. Abercrombie will soon be at hand."

"And I am surprised that you should await him. I judge that he has sufficient force to overwhelm you."

"We are never beaten before battle. The Marquis de Montcalm would not stay, unless he had a fair chance of success."

Robert was silent and St. Luc quickly went back to his work. All day the men toiled, and when the sun went down, they were still at their task. The ring of axes and the crash of falling trees resounded through the dark. Part of the soldiers put their kettles and pots on the fires, but the others labored on. In the night came the valiant De Levis with his men, and Montcalm gave him a heartfelt welcome. De Levis was a host in himself, and Montcalm felt that he was just in time. He expected the battle on the morrow. His scouts told him that Abercrombie would be at hand, but without his artillery. The Marquis looked at the formidable abattis, the rows and rows of trees, presenting their myriad of spiked ends, and hope was alive in his heart. He regretted once more the absence of the Indians who had been led away by the sulky Tandakora, but victory, won with their help, demanded a fearful price, as he had learned at William Henry.

Montcalm, St. Luc, De Levis, Bourlamaque, Lotbiniére and other trusted officers held a consultation far in the night. An important event had occurred already. A scouting force of French and Canadians under Trepezec and Langy had been trapped by rangers under Rogers and troops under Fitch and Lyman. The French and Canadians were cut to pieces, but in the battle the gallant young Lord Howe, the real leader of the Anglo-American army, had been killed. He had gone forward with the vanguard, exposing himself rashly, perhaps, and his life was the forfeit. Immediate confusion in the Anglo-American councils followed, and Montcalm and his lieutenants had noticed the lack of precision and directness.

Robert did not see the French officers going to the council, but he knew that the French army meant to stay. Even while the men were cutting down the trees he could not persuade himself wholly that Montcalm would fight there at Ticonderoga, but as the night advanced his last faint doubt disappeared. He would certainly witness a great battle on the morrow.

He could not sleep. Every nerve in him seemed to be alive. One vivid picture after another floated before his mind. The lake behind him grew dim. Before him were the camp fires of the French, the wooden wall, the dark line of the forest and hills, and the crest of Defiance looking solemnly down on them. Although held firmly there, within lines which one could not pass, nobody seemed to take any notice of him. He could rest or watch as he chose, and he had no choice but to watch.

He saw the French lie down on their arms, save for the numerous sentinels posted everywhere, and after a while, though most of the night was gone, the ring of axes and the fall of trees ceased. There was a hum of voices but that too died in time, and long after midnight, with his back against a tree, he dozed a little while.

He was awakened by a premonition, a warning out of the dark, and opening his eyes he saw Garay slinking near. He did not know whether the spy meant another attempt upon his life, but, standing up, he stared at him intently. Garay shrank away and disappeared in the further ranges of the camp. Robert somehow was not afraid. The man would not make such a trial again at so great a risk, and his mind turned back to its preoccupation, the great battle that was coming.

Near morning he dozed again for an hour or so, but he awoke before the summer dawn. All his faculties were alive, and his body attuned when he saw the sun rise, bringing with it the momentous day.

CHAPTER XIV.
TICONDEROGA

The French army rose with the sun, the drums beating the call to battle. Montcalm stationed the battalions of Languedoc and La Sarre on the left with Bourlamaque to command them, on the right De Levis led the battalions of Béarn, Guienne and La Reine. Montcalm himself stood with the battalion of Royal Roussillon in the center, and St. Luc was by his side. Volunteers held the sunken ground between the breastwork and the outlet of Lake George, a strong force of regulars and Canadians was on the side of Lake Champlain under the guns of the fort there. Then, having taken their places, all the parts of the army went to work again, strengthening the defenses with ax and spade, improving every moment that might be left.

All thought of escape left Robert's mind in the mighty and thrilling drama that was about to be played before him. Once more he stared at the long line of the lake, and then his whole attention was for the circling forest, and the hills. That was where the army of his country lay. Nothing was to be expected from the lake. Victory would come from the woods, and he looked so long at the trees that they blurred together into one mass. He knew that the English and Americans were near, but just how near he could not gather from those around him.

He brushed his eyes to clear them, and continued to study the forest. The sun, great and brilliant, was flooding it with light, gilding the slopes and crests of Defiance, and tinging the green of the leaves with gold. Nothing stirred there. The wilderness seemed silent, as if men never fought in its depths. Time went slowly on. After all, the army might not advance to the attack that day. If so, his disappointment would be bitter. He wanted a great victory, and he wanted it at once.

His eyes suddenly caught a gleam on the crest of Defiance. A bit of red flashed among the trees. He thought it was the uniform of a British soldier, and his heart beat hard. The army was surely advancing, the attack would be made, and the victory would be won that day, not on the morrow nor next week, but before the sun set.

The blood pounded in his temples. He looked at the French. They, too, had seen the scarlet gleam on Defiance and they were watching. Montcalm and St. Luc began to talk together earnestly. De Levis and Bourlamaque walked back and forth among their troops, but their gaze was upon the crest. The men lay down ax and spade for the time, and reached for their arms. Robert saw the sunlight glittering on musket and bayonet, and once more he thrilled at the thought of the great drama on which the curtain was now rising.

Another scarlet patch appeared on the crest and then more. He knew that the scouts and skirmishers were there, doubtless in strong force. It was likely that the rangers, who would be in forest green, were more numerous than the English, and the attack could not now be far away. A sharp crack, a puff of white smoke on the hill, and the first shot of Ticonderoga was fired. Then came a volley, but the French made no reply. None of the bullets had reached them. Robert did not know it then, but the gleam came from the red blankets of Iroquois Indians, the allies of the English, and not from English uniforms. They kept up a vigorous but harmless fire for a short while, and then drew off.

Silence descended once more on the forest, and Robert was puzzled. It could not be possible that this was to be the only attack. The smoke of the rifles was already drifting away from the crest, gone like summer vapor. The French were returning to their work with ax and spade. The forest covered and enclosed everything. No sound came from it. Montcalm and St. Luc, walking up and down, began to talk together again. They looked no longer toward the crest of Defiance, but watched the southern wilderness.

The work with the ax increased. Montcalm had no mind to lose the precious hours. More trees fell fast, and they were added to the formidable works. The sun grew hotter and poured down sheaves of fiery rays, but the toilers disregarded it, swinging the axes with muscles that took no note of weariness. Robert thought the morning would last forever. An hour before noon De Galissonnière was passing, and, noticing him sitting on a low mound, he said:

"I did not know what had become of you, Mr. Lennox, but I see that you, like ourselves, await the battle."

"So I do," said Robert as lightly as he could, "but it seems to me that it's somewhat delayed."

"Not our fault, I assure you. Perhaps you didn't think so earlier, but you see we're willing to fight, no matter how great the odds."

"I admit it. The Marquis de Montcalm has his courage—perhaps too much."

De Galissonnière glanced at the strong works, and his smile was confident, but he merely said:

"It is for the future to tell."

Then he went on, and Robert hoped that whatever happened the battle would spare the young Frenchman.

Up went the sun toward the zenith. A light wind rustled the foliage. Noon was near, and he began to wonder anew what had become of the advancing army. Suddenly, the echo of a crash came out of the forest in front. He stood erect, listening intently, and the sound rose again, but it was not an echo now. It was real, and he knew that the battle was at hand.

The crashes became continuous. Mingled with them were shouts, and a cloud of smoke began to float above the trees. The French fired a cannon as a signal, and, before the echoes of its report rolled away, every man dropped ax or spade, and was in his place, weapon in hand. The noise of the firing in front grew fast. Montcalm's scouts and pickets were driven in, and the soldiers of the advancing army began to show among the trees. The French batteries opened. The roar in Robert's ear was terrific, but he stood at his utmost height in order that he might see the assault. His eyes caught the gleam of uniforms and the flash of sunlight on bayonet and rifle. He knew now that his own people, dauntless and tenacious, were coming. He did not know that they had left their artillery behind, and that they expected to destroy the French army with bayonet and rifle and musket.

The fire from the French barrier increased in volume. Its crash beat heavily and continuously on the drums of Robert's ears. A deadly sleet was beating upon the advancing English and Americans. Already their dead were heaping up in rows. Montcalm's men showed their heads only above their works, their bodies were sheltered by the logs and they fired and fired into the charging masses until the barrels of rifles and muskets grew too hot for them to hold. Meanwhile they shouted with all their might: "Vive la France! Vive notre General! Vive le Roi!" and St. Luc, who stood always with Montcalm, hummed softly and under his breath: "Hier, sur le pont d'Avignon, j'ai oui chanter la belle."

"It goes well," he said to Montcalm.

"Aye, a fair beginning," replied the Marquis.

Fire ran through French veins. No cannon balls were coming from the enemy to sweep down their defenses. Bullets from rifle and musket were beating in vain on their wooden wall, and before them came the foe, a vast, converging mass, a target that no one could miss. They were far from their own land, deep in the great North American wilderness, but as they saw it, they fought for the honor and glory of France, and to keep what was hers. They redoubled their shouts and fired faster and faster. A great cloud of smoke rose over the clearing and the forest, but through it the attacking army always advanced, a hedge of bayonets leading.

Robert saw everything clearly. His heart sank for a moment, and then leaped up again. Many of his own had fallen, but a great red curve was advancing. It was the British regulars, the best troops in the charge that Europe could furnish, and they would surely carry the wooden wall. As far as he could see, in front and to left and right, their bayonets flashed in the sun, and a cry of admiration sprang to his lips. Forward they came, their line even and beautiful, and then the tempest beat upon them. The entire French fire was concentrated upon the concave red lines. The batteries poured grape shot upon them and a sleet of lead cut through flesh and bone. Gaps were torn in their ranks, but the others closed up, and came on, the American Colonials on their flanks charging as bravely.

Robert suddenly remembered a vision of his, vague and fleeting then, but very real now. He was standing here at Ticonderoga, looking at the battle as it passed before him, and now it was no vision, but the truth. Had Tayoga's Manitou opened the future to him for a moment? Then the memory was gone and the terrific drama of the present claimed his whole mind.

The red lines were not stopped. In the face of awful losses they were still coming. They were among the trees where the men were entangled with the boughs or ran upon the wooden spikes. Often they tripped and fell, but rising they returned to the charge, offering their breasts to the deadly storm that never diminished for an instant.

Robert walked back and forth in his little space. Every nerve was on edge. The smoke of the firing was in eye, throat and nostril, and his brain was hot. But confidence was again supreme. "They'll come! They'll come! Nothing can stop them!" he kept repeating to himself.

Now the Colonials on the flank pressed forward, and they also advanced through the lines of the regulars in front and charged with them. Together British and Americans climbed over the mass of fallen trees in face of the terrible fire, and reached the wooden wall itself, where the sleet beat directly upon their faces. For a long distance behind them, their dead and wounded lay in hundreds and hundreds.

Many of them tried to scale the barrier, but were beaten back. Now Montcalm, St. Luc, De Levis, Bourlamaque and all the French leaders made their mightiest efforts. The eye of the French commander swept the field. He neglected nothing. Never was a man better served by his lieutenants. St. Luc was at every threatened point, encouraging with voice and example. Bourlamaque received a dangerous wound, but refused to quit the field. Bougainville was hit, but his hurt was less severe, and he took no notice of it, two bullets pierced the hat of De Levis, St. Luc took a half dozen through his clothes and his body was grazed three times, but his gay and warlike spirit mounted steadily, and he hummed his little French air over and over again.

More British and Americans pressed to the wooden wall. The new Black Watch, stalwart Scotchmen, bagpipes playing, charged over everything. Two British columns made a powerful and tremendous attack upon the French right, where stood the valiant battalions of Béarn and Guienne. It seemed, for a while, that they might overwhelm everything. They were against the barrier itself, and were firing into the defense. Montcalm rushed to the spot with all the reserves he could muster. St. Luc sprang among the men and shouted to them to increase their fire. This point became the center of the battle, and its full fury was concentrated there. A mass of Highlanders, tearing at the wooden wall, refused to give back. Though they fell fast, a captain climbed up the barrier. Officers and men followed him. They stood a moment on the crest as if to poise themselves, and then leaped down among the French, where they were killed. Those who stood on the other side were swept by a hurricane of fire, and at last they yielded slowly.

Robert saw all, and he was seized with a great horror. The army was not crashing over everything. Those who entered the French works died there. The wooden wall held. Nowhere was the line of defense broken. Boats loaded with troops coming down the outlet of Lake George to turn the French left were repelled by the muskets of the Canadian volunteers. Some of the boats were sunk, and the soldiers struggled in the water, as cannon balls and bullets beat upon them.

His view of the field was blurred, for a while, by the smoke from so much firing, which floated in thickening clouds over all the open spaces and the edges of the forest. It produced curious optical illusions. The French loomed through it, increased fourfold in numbers, every individual man magnified in size. He saw them lurid and gigantic, pulling the triggers of their rifles or muskets, or working the batteries. The cannon also grew from twelve-pounders or eighteen-pounders into guns three or four times as large, and many stood where none had stood before.

The smoke continued to inflame his brain also, and it made him pass through great alternations of hope and fear. Now the army was going to sweep over the wooden wall in spite of everything. With sheer weight and bravery it would crush the French and take Ticonderoga. It must be. Because he wanted it to be, it was going to be. Then he passed to the other extreme. When one of the charges spent itself at the barrier, sending perhaps a few men over it, like foam from a wave that has reached its crest, his heart sank to the depths, and he was sure the British and Americans could not come again. Mortal men would not offer themselves so often to slaughter. If the firing died for a little space he was in deep despair, but his soul leaped up again as the charge came anew. It was certainly victory this time. Hope could not be crushed in him. His vivid fancy made him hear above the triumphant shouts of the French the deep cheers of the advancing army, the beating of drums and the playing of invisible bands.

All the time, whether in attack or retreat, the smoke continued to increase and to inflame and excite. It was like a gas, its taste was acrid and bitter as death. Robert coughed and tried to blow it away, but it returned in waves heavier than ever, and then he ceased to fight against it.

The British and American troops came again and again to the attack, their officers leading them on. Never had they shown greater courage or more willingness to die. When the first lines were cut down at the barrier, others took their places. They charged into the vast mass of fallen trees and against the spikes. Blinded by the smoke of so much firing, they nevertheless kept their faces toward the enemy and sought to see him. The fierce cheering of the French merely encouraged them to new attempts.

The battle went on for hours. It seemed days to Robert. Mass after mass of British and Colonials continued to charge upon the wooden wall, always to be broken down by the French fire, leaving heaps of their dead among those logs and boughs and on that bristling array of spikes. At last they advanced no more, twilight came over the field, the terrible fire that had raged since noon died, and the sun set upon the greatest military triumph ever won by France in the New World.

Twilight gathered over the most sanguinary field America had yet seen. In the east the dark was already at hand, but in the west the light from the sunken sun yet lingered, casting a scarlet glow alike over the fallen and the triumphant faces of the victors. Within the works where the French had stood fires were lighted, and everything there was brilliant, but outside, where so much valor had been wasted, the shadows that seemed to creep out of the illimitable forest grew thicker and thicker.

The wind moaned incessantly among the leaves, and the persistent smoke that had been so bitter in the throat and nostrils of Robert still hung in great clouds that the wind moved but little. From the woods came long, fierce howls. The wolves, no longer frightened by the crash of cannon and muskets, were coming, and under cover of bushes and floating smoke, they crept nearer and nearer.

Robert sat a long time, bewildered, stunned. The incredible had happened. He had seen it with his own eyes, and yet it was hard to believe that it was true. The great Anglo-American army had been beaten by a French force far less in numbers. Rather, it had beaten itself. That neglect to bring up the cannon had proved fatal, and the finest force yet gathered on the soil of North America had been cut to pieces. A prodigious opportunity had been lost by a commander who stayed a mile and a half in the rear, while his valiant men charged to certain death.

Young Lennox walked stiffly a few steps. No one paid any attention to him. In the dark, and amid the joyous excitement of the defenders, he might have been taken for a Frenchman. But he made no attempt, then, to escape. No such thought was in his mind for the moment. His amazement gave way to horror. He wanted to see what was beyond the wooden wall where he knew the dead and wounded lay, piled deep among the logs and sharpened boughs. Unbelievable it was, but it was true. His own eyes had seen and his own ears had heard. He listened to the triumphant shouts of the French, and his soul sank within him.

A few shots came from the forest now and then, but the great army had vanished, save for its fallen. Montcalm, still cautious, relaxing no vigilance, fearing that the enemy would yet come back with his cannon, walked among his troops and gave them thanks in person. Beer and wine in abundance, and food were served to them. Fires were lighted and the field that they had defended was to be their camp. Many scouts were sent into the forest to see what had become of the opposing army. Most of the soldiers, after eating and drinking, threw themselves upon the ground and slept, but it was long before the leader and any of his lieutenants closed their eyes. Although he felt a mighty joy over his great victory of the day, Montcalm was still a prey to anxieties. His own force, triumphant though it might be, was small. The enemy might come again on the morrow with nearly four to one, and, if he brought his cannon with him, he could take Ticonderoga, despite the great losses he had suffered already. Once more he talked with St. Luc, whom he trusted implicitly.

The Chevalier did not believe a second attack would be made, and his belief was so strong it amounted to a conviction.

"The same mind," he said, "that sent their army against us without artillery, will now go to the other extreme. Having deemed us negligible it will think us invincible."

St. Luc's logic was correct. The French passed the night in peace, and the next morning, when De Levis went out with a strong party to look for the enemy he found that he was gone, and that in his haste he had left behind vast quantities of food and other supplies which the French eagerly seized. Montcalm that day, full of pride, caused a great cross to be erected on his victorious field of battle and upon it he wrote in Latin:

"Quid dux? quid miles? quid strata ingentia ligna? En Signum! en victor! Deus hic, Deus ipse triumphat."

Which a great American writer has translated into:

"Soldier and chief and ramparts' strength are nought; Behold the conquering cross! 'Tis God the triumph wrought."

But for Robert the night that closed down was the blackest he had ever known. It had never occurred to him that Abercrombie's army could be defeated. Confident in its overwhelming numbers, he had believed that it would easily sweep away the French and take Ticonderoga. The skill and valor of Montcalm, St. Luc, De Levis and the others, no matter how skillful and valiant they might be, could avail nothing, and, after Ticonderoga, it would be a mere question of time until Crown Point fell too. And after that would come Quebec and the conquest of Canada.

Now, when his spirits had soared so high, the fall was correspondingly low. His sensitive mind, upon which events always painted themselves with such vividness, reflected only the darkest pictures. He saw the triumphant advance of the French, the Indians laying waste the whole of New York Province, and the enemy at the gates of New York itself.

The night itself was a perfect reproduction of his own mind. He saw through his spirits as through a glass. The dusk was thick, heavy, it was noisome, it had a quality that was almost ponderable, it was unpleasant to eye and nostril, he tasted and breathed the smoke that was shot through it, and he felt a sickening of the soul. He heard a wind moaning through the forest, and it was to him a dirge, the lament of those who had fallen.

He knew there had been no lack of bravery on the part of his own. After a while he took some consolation in that fact. British and Americans had come to the attack long after hope of success was gone. They had not known how to win, but never had men known better how to die. Such valor would march to triumph in the end.

He lay awake almost the whole night, and he did not expect Abercrombie to advance again. Somehow he had the feeling that the play, so far as this particular drama was concerned, was played out. The blow was so heavy that he was in a dull and apathetic state from which he was stirred only once in the evening, and that was when two Frenchmen passed near him, escorting a prisoner of whose face he caught a glimpse in the firelight. He started forward, exclaiming:

"Charteris!"[1]

The young man, tall, handsome and firm of feature, although a captive, turned.

"Who called me?" he asked.

"It is I, Robert Lennox," said Robert. "I knew you in New York!"

"Aye, Mr. Lennox. I recognize you now. We meet again, after so long a time. I could have preferred the meeting to be elsewhere and under other circumstances, but it is something to know that you are alive."

They shook hands with great friendliness and the Frenchmen, who were guarding Charteris, waited patiently.

"May our next meeting be under brighter omens," said Robert.

"I think it will be," said Charteris confidently.

Then he went on. It was a long time before they were to see each other again, and the drama that was to bring them face to face once more was destined to be as thrilling as that at Ticonderoga.

The next night came heavy and dark, and Robert, who continued to be treated with singular forbearance, wandered toward Lake Champlain, which lay pale and shadowy under the thick dusk. No one stopped him. The sentinels seemed to have business elsewhere, and suddenly he remembered his old threat to escape. Hope returned to a mind that had been stunned for a time, and it came back vivid and strong. Then hope sank down again, when a figure issued from the dusk, and stood before him. It was St. Luc.

"Mr. Lennox," said the Chevalier, "what are you doing here?"

"Merely wandering about," replied Robert. "I'm a prisoner, as you know, but no one is bothering about me, which I take to be natural when the echoes of so great a battle have scarcely yet died."

St. Luc looked at him keenly and Robert met his gaze. He could not read the eye of the Chevalier.

"You have been a prisoner of ours once before, but you escaped," said the Chevalier. "It seems that you are a hard lad to hold."

"But then I had the help of the greatest trailer and forest runner in the world, my staunch friend, Tayoga, the Onondaga."

"If he rescued you once he will probably try to do it again, and the great hunter, Willet, is likely to be with him. I suppose you were planning a few moments ago to escape along the shore of the lake."

"I might have been, but I see now that it is too late."

"Too late is a phrase that should be seldom used by youth."

Robert tried once again to read the Chevalier's eye, but St. Luc's look contained the old enigma.

"I admit," said young Lennox, "that I thought I might find an open place in your line. It was only a possible chance."

St. Luc shrugged his shoulders, and looked at the darkness that lay before them like a great black blanket.

"There is much yet to be done by us at Ticonderoga," he said. "Perhaps it is true that a possible chance for you to escape does exist, but my duties are too important for me to concern myself about guarding a single prisoner."

His figure vanished. He was gone without noise, and Robert stared at the place where he had been. Then the hope of escape came back, more vivid and more powerful than ever. "Too late," was a phrase that should not be known to youth. St. Luc was right. He walked straight ahead. No sentinel barred the way. Presently the lake, still and luminous, stretched across his path, and, darting into the bushes along its edge, he ran for a long time. Then he sank down and looked back. He saw dimly the lights of the camp, but he heard no sound of pursuit.

Rising, he began a great curve about Ticonderoga, intending to seek his own army, which he knew could not yet be far away. Once he heard light footsteps and hid deep in the bush. From his covert he saw a band of warriors at least twenty in number go by, their lean, sinewy figures showing faintly in the dusk. Their faces were turned toward the south and he shuddered. Already they were beginning to raid the border. He knew that they had taken little or no part in the battle at Ticonderoga, but now the great success of the French would bring them flocking back to Montcalm's banner, and they would rush like wolves upon those whom they thought defenseless, hoping for more slaughters like that of William Henry.

Tandakora would not neglect such a glowing opportunity for scalps. His savage spirit would incite the warriors to attempts yet greater, and Robert looked closely at the dusky line, thinking for a moment that he might be there. But he did not see his gigantic figure and the warriors flitted on, gone like shadows in the darkness. Then the fugitive youth resumed his own flight.

Far in the night Robert sank down in a state of exhaustion. It was a physical and mental collapse, coming with great suddenness, but he recognized it for what it was, the natural consequence flowing from a period of such excessive strain. His emotions throughout the great battle had been tense and violent, and they had been hardly less so in the time that followed and in the course of the events that led to his escape. And knowing, he forced himself to do what was necessary.

He lay down in the shelter of dense bushes, and kept himself perfectly quiet for a long time. He would not allow hand or foot to move. His weary heart at last began to beat with regularity, the blood ceased to pound in his temples, and his nerves grew steadier. He dozed a little, or at least passed into a state that was midway between wakefulness and oblivion. Then the terrible battle was fought once more before him. Again he heard the crash and roar of the French fire, again he saw British and Americans coming forward in indomitable masses, offering themselves to death, once again he saw them tangled among the logs and sharpened boughs, and then mowed down at the wooden wall.

He roused himself and passed his hands over his eyes to shut away that vision of the stricken field and the vivid reminder of his terrible disappointment. The picture was still as fresh as the reality and it sent shudders through him every time he saw it. He would keep it from his sight whenever he could, lest he grow too morbid.

He rose and started once more toward the south, but the forest became more dense and tangled and the country rougher. In his weakened state he was not able to think with his usual clearness and precision, and he lost the sense of direction. He began to wander about aimlessly, and at last he stopped almost in despair.

He was in a desperate plight. He was unarmed, and a man alone and without weapons in the wilderness was usually as good as lost. He looked around, trying to study the points of the compass. The night was not dark. Trees and bushes stood up distinctly, and on a bough not far away, his eyes suddenly caught a flash of blue.

The flash was made by a small, glossy bird that wavered on a bough, and he was about to turn away, taking no further notice of it, when the bird flew slowly before him and in a direction which he now knew led straight toward the south. He remembered. Back to his mind rushed an earlier escape, and how he had followed the flight of a bird to safety. Had Tayoga's Manitou intervened again in his favor? Was it chance? Or did he in a dazed state imagine that he saw what he did not see?

The bird, an azure flash, flew on before him, and hope flowing in an invincible tide in his veins, he followed. He was in continual fear lest the blue flame fade away, but on he went, over hills and across valleys and brooks, and it was always just before him. He had been worn and weary before, but now he felt strong and active. Courage rose steadily in his veins, and he had no doubt that he would reach friends.

Near dawn the bird suddenly disappeared among the leaves. Robert stopped and heard a light foot-step in the bushes. Being apprehensive lest he be re-taken, he shrank away and then stopped. He listened a while, and the sound not being repeated, he hoped that he had been mistaken, but a voice called suddenly from a bush not ten feet away:

"Come, Dagaeoga! The Great Bear and I await you. Tododaho, watching on his star, has sent us into your path."

Robert, uttering a joyful cry, sprang forward, and the Onondaga and Willet, rising from the thicket, greeted him with the utmost warmth.

"I knew we'd find you again," said Willet "How did you manage to escape?"

"A way seemed to open for me," replied Robert. "The last man I saw in the French camp was St. Luc. After that I met no sentinel, although I passed where a sentinel would stand."

"Ah!" said Willet.

They gave him food, and after sunrise they started toward the south. Robert told how he had seen the great battle and the French victory.

"Tayoga, Black Rifle, Grosvenor and I were in the attack," said Willet, "but we went through it without a scratch. No troops ever fought more bravely than ours. The defeat was the fault of the commander, not theirs. But we'll put behind us the battle lost and think of the battle yet to be won."

"So we will," said Robert, as he looked around at the great curving forest, its deep green tinted with the light brown of summer. It was a friendly forest now. It no longer had the aspect of the night before, when the wolves, their jaws slavering in anticipation, howled in its thickets. Rabbits sprang up as they passed, but the little creatures of the wild did not seem to be afraid. They did not run away. Instead, they crouched under the bushes, and gazed with mild eyes at the human beings who made no threats. A deer, drinking at the edge of a brook, raised its head a little and then continued to drink. Birds sang in the dewy dawn with uncommon freshness and sweetness. The whole world was renewed.

Creature, as he was, of his moods, Robert's spirits soared again at his meeting with Tayoga and Willet, those staunch friends of his, bound to him by such strong ties and so many dangers shared. The past was the past, Ticonderoga was a defeat, a great defeat, when a victory had been expected, but it was not irreparable. Hope sang in his heart and his face flushed in the dawn. The Onondaga, looking at him, smiled.

"Dagaeoga already looks to the future," he said.

"So I do," replied Robert with enthusiasm. "Why shouldn't I? The night just passed has favored me. I escaped. I met you and Dave, and it's a glorious morning."

The sun was rising in a splendid sea of color, tinting the woods with red and gold. Never had the wilderness looked more beautiful to him. He turned his face in the direction of Ticonderoga.

"We'll come back," he said, his heart full of courage, "and we'll yet win the victory, even to the taking of Quebec."

"So we will," said the hunter.

"Aye, Stadacona itself will fall," said Tayoga.

Refreshed and strong, they plunged anew into the forest, traveling swiftly toward the south.

[Footnote 1: The story of Edward Charteris and his adventures at Ticonderoga and Quebec is told in the author's novel, "A Soldier of Manhattan."]

THE END